BRITISH RAILWAYS

PAST and PRESENT

No 58

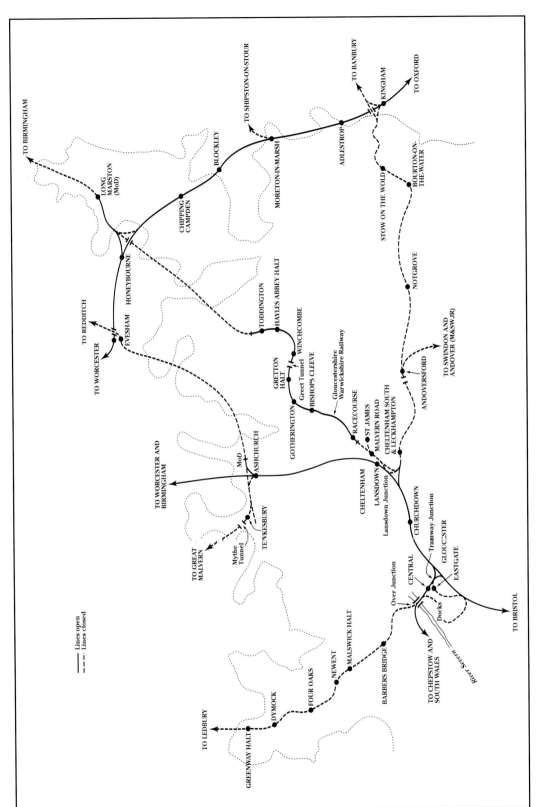

Map of the area covered by this book, showing locations featured or referred to in the text.

BRITISH RAILWAYS

PAST and PRESENT

No 58

North Gloucestershire

John Stretton

Past and
Present

Past & Present Publishing Ltd

First published in 2008

British Library Cataloguing in Publication Data

A catalogue record for this book is available from the British Library.

ISBN 978 1 85895 257 4

Past & Present Publishing Ltd
The Trundle
Ringstead Road
Great Addington
Kettering
Northants NN14 4BW

Tel/Fax: 01536 330588
email: sales@nostalgiacollection.com
Website: www.nostalgiacollection.com

Printed and bound in the Czech Republic

ACKNOWLEDGEMENTS

As ever, I am indebted to a wide variety and number of people who have assisted in one way or another. Photographers, especially, have been very willing to submit their images for consideration and I am truly grateful to those who aided in this way – without them and their foresight in pointing the camera at strategic moments the book would have struggled to be born! They are duly credited throughout the collection, but I take this opportunity to offer all of them my profound gratitude. In addition, there are those who have helped me before and have been fool enough to put their name in the frame again! Among all of these there are some who deserve especial mention, and I would like to here present my sincere thanks to: Bryan Nicholls and Savita (for proof reading and courtesy); Ben Ashworth and Trevor Owen (for entrusting their priceless images to my care!); John Edgington; Edwin Wilmshurst; Richard Casserley; Roger Carpenter; the Gloucestershire Warwickshire Railway for lineside access; and, not least, Brian Smith and Sharon Rich for their interest, encouragement and support. Finally, as usual, thanks go to all at Silver Link – Peter for encouragement and for putting up with changes of plan and countless phone calls; David for his unflinching patience and courtesy; and to Will and Mick for their usual skilful and speedy editing and design. Thank you all! The illustrations credited 'MJS' are mine.

CONTENTS

ASHCHURCH: Those were the days, my friend! In these days of fewer freight duties, vacuum-fitted, and predominantly handled by the ubiquitous Class 66s, what wouldn't we give to relive sights such as this? At 7.10pm on the evening of Saturday 6 June 1959, during the photographer's first visit to the site, he has captured the delightful scene at Ashchurch of diminutive No 43210 trundling north on an unfitted mixed freight. Carriages of a train for Evesham can just be seen on the extreme left. Happily, in 2007, after some years in the wilderness, Ashchurch is again on the railway map, but all that is common today to this scene are the tracks and the tall conifer! *Michael Mensing*

Above ASHCHURCH was unique on the ex-MR Birmingham-Bristol main line in having a flat crossing. The single track served as a direct link between the two branches that curved sharply east and west from the station, to Evesham and Tewkesbury. Looking west towards the latter, No 43046 runs over the crossing to reach the Evesham tracks on 21 March 1957. Less than eight years old at this time, the locomotive had been a Saltley (21A) incumbent since the previous November, but would move north to Manchester and the North East until withdrawal from Lostock Hall. Note the large water tower to the right; this still stands proudly in 2007, surrounded by new developments! *John Edgington*

Below CHELTENHAM SPA: While obviously a more modern picture, this is still a view that is no longer the norm. Long-distance and/or cross-country trains are no longer loco-hauled, except in emergencies, but on 5 June 1993 this view of InterCity-liveried No 47839 at the head of a rake of similarly decorated coaches, less than a year before Privatisation, was attractive but far from unorthodox. Named *Pride of Saltley* for just nine months in 2002 (then *Pegasus* in September 2006), the locomotive was still active in 2007, as an asset of Riviera Trains and based at Carlisle Kingmoor. Here, with no specific allocation, it heads the 1005 York-Paignton InterCity Holidaymaker. *MJS*

INTRODUCTION

I have been privileged to author several 'British Railways Past and Present' volumes for this publisher, both in the main series and the 'Companion' series, and all have been a pleasure to produce, despite the occasional problems in attempting to stand in the shoes of the original photographers – but this one is different! It is the third in the main series with which I have been entrusted – the others being Leicestershire and a second volume on Oxfordshire – but it is the first county that I have had to split into more than one part. This in itself has been both a trial and a pleasure, as the size of the county has dictated more mileage, but availability of more page space has enabled me to do greater justice to the many and varied locations within Gloucestershire and to have the honour of displaying many more wonderful illustrations from past cameramen (and they are, sadly, all men!).

In preparing the three volumes, I have 'sliced' the county into roughly horizontal sections, the first covering the area north of a line east and west from the city of Gloucester. Volume 3 – South Gloucestershire – will draw a line westwards from Badminton to the Severn Tunnel and cover the railways south thereof, and Volume 2 – Central Gloucestershire – will take the chunk between, on both sides of the Severn. The former Severn & Wye lines north from Severn Bridge into the Forest of Dean will not be featured, despite being within the county boundary, as they have already been extensively covered in my two volumes on the Dean Forest Railway in the 'Past and Present Companion' series.

As those who know me will be aware, I do not like re-using images previously included in any other publication (or, indeed, widely available elsewhere) and, as with my previous offerings, I have trawled extensively to find nuggets that have not previously enjoyed the glare of publicity! Many willing photographers and collection custodians have helped me in my search, and are readily acknowledged and appreciated.

Much has happened over the years since rails first began appearing in Gloucestershire and there have been varying fortunes for routes and individual locations – relevant details accompany the captions. This has meant much research in preparation and careful examination on the ground to create as meaningful a 'then and now' comparison as possible. We often decry the desecration of our natural heritage by modern living and its attendant development, but I am constantly amazed – and sometimes thwarted! – by the growth of bushes and trees over the years. There are also places where some item of railway presence has survived against all the odds. As with many of my previous contributions to the ongoing 'Past and Present' series, there have been occasions when I have perforce moved left, right, forward or backward to attempt any sort of recreation, and where this does slightly detract from an exact recreation, I beg the reader's indulgence. To those who may feel less than wholly satisfied, I merely say, 'You try it!'

Those areas of our railway system that survive have seen much change over their long history, sometimes even in short time spans, and I have tried to portray some of this change in the ensuing pages; where the tracks have disappeared completely, I have attempted to make the resultant image as interesting and attractive as possible. I have thoroughly enjoyed 'going back in time' and wallowing in nostalgia, and I hope that you will equally enjoy this journey and that it may encourage you to investigate locations for yourself. This also applies to non-railway areas of life, and I encourage all to take a camera and record the scenes for yourself. After all, if those far-sighted individuals who have captured the past for us in this book had put their cameras away, we would have lost so much!

The images have been carefully chosen and I hope you will excuse the occasional diversion from a strict 'past and present' comparison. As with my other books, if anyone finds errors, or would like to add to the well of knowledge plumbed for the book – or, indeed, would like to pass on any messages and/or comments about the collection – I would be pleased to hear from them via the publisher. Any errors are mine alone and I would like any to be corrected in time for any possible future reprint. I abhor the thought of inaccuracies being perpetuated by me and possibly repeated by future historians. Thank you.

We are fortunate that there were – and still are – skilful, dedicated and energetic photographers who thought nothing of travelling the length and breadth of the UK capturing images on film. There are undoubtedly more views of the railways of the county 'out there'. Again, I would be delighted to hear of any, especially from those who have not had their work previously published. Finally, by all means use this book as a sort of travel guide. Go out and enjoy yourselves!

Gloucester Central

GLOUCESTER CENTRAL: Perhaps not surprisingly, we begin our journey at Gloucester. Once home to two main-line stations – Central (GWR) and Eastgate (MR/LMS) – this was reduced to just one in 1975, with the closure of Eastgate. Thereafter, all trains were concentrated on Central, but even this has not prevented a reduction in status, with Virgin trains eschewing the resultant reversals and bypassing the station completely. In happier times, on 7 November 1963, Central is enjoying a busy spell. No 4564, on the right, waits for the road, while 'Hall' No 6993 *Arthog* Hall slowly makes its way along the up through road, behind a freight, and a mixed rake of stock is shunted in the far platform. The gentleman reading his newspaper appears oblivious to it all.

By comparison, the present-day station is spartan, as the old arched awning and supporting columns have been swept away, replaced by a more utilitarian, single-span affair. Similarly, this western end of the station complex sees little traffic compared with its eastern arm, with the amount of freight and through traffic much reduced and previous western branches having closed. On 11 July 2007 one of the few remaining through passenger services is seen leaving past the ever-spreading trackbed weeds. No 170109 is heading away with 1V18, the 1002 Central Trains Nottingham-Cardiff Central cross-country service. Note that the bay platform on the left is still in use, but now as No 3 rather than No 1.
Ben Ashworth/MJS

GLOUCESTER CENTRAL: Again looking westwards, a mixed ballast train, with appropriate lamp headcode, moves slowly into the station complex behind No 5252 on 22 August 1964. Built as one of the 151 '4200' Class 2-8-0Ts, No 5252 was one of the 'super' variety, introduced from 1923, with enlarged cylinders and other detail differences and designated 8F, as opposed to the 7F of its predecessors. Allocated to Newport (Pill) shed at Nationalisation in 1948, it remained a South Wales loco until withdrawal, which came at Aberdare in May 1965. A very neat and tidy picture.

Moments earlier, 'Manor' No 7814 *Fringford Manor* stood slightly ahead of No 5252, awaiting its next turn of duty. New from Swindon Works in January 1939, its first allocation was to Westbury shed. By Nationalisation it had reached Bristol (Bath Road), but a move to Laira soon followed and thereafter the loco was a true wanderer. Reading, Newton Abbot and Cardiff (Canton) were all homes before a move to Machynlleth came in February 1959, ready for the summer season over Cambrian Coast metals. 1963 saw allocation to three South Wales sheds, before moves to Gloucester (Horton Road), Didcot and back to Gloucester, where the axe fell on 19 September 1965. The end came swiftly, later that month at Bird's scrapyard at Long Marston. Allocated to the local shed, as seen here, note the beginning of the end in the form of the absence of a front number plate and a mere chalked number on the buffer beam. Happily, it still retains its name and cabside numberplate. Note also the elaborate rooftop of the station, now sadly gone.

A week on from the previous picture, on 29 August 1964, our intrepid photographer is back again at Central station and again enjoying glorious summer sunshine. This delightful portrait shows 9F No 92243 on a heavily loaded coke train. New in October 1958 – when diesels were being built in increasing numbers and the writing was on the wall for steam traction – its first allocation was to Newport (Ebbw Junction) shed. The 9F lasted just seven years and three months, but served six different sheds in that time! The end was at Bristol (Barrow Road) shed on 15 January 1966, a criminal waste of a nearly new valuable asset, and of taxpayers' money! The engine is here blowing off, presumably stopped from immediate progress, and the fireman peers from his cab, checking the signals ahead. The ex-GWR tender engine in the distance stands on the bridge over London Road. *All Gerald Adams, MJS collection*

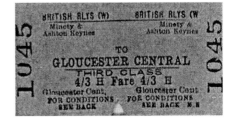

GLOUCESTER CENTRAL: 'Has the photographer nothing better to do than point his camera at us?' seems to be the thought, judging by the driver's expression! Sitting in Platform 1, the bay at the western end of the station, No 4573 quietly simmers and the carriage door stands open, as the train bound for the Ledbury branch awaits departure. New in November 1924, last but one of the original design of these 4MT 2-6-2Ts with straight side tanks, No 4573 went to Westbury shed, where it stayed until 2 October 1953. Worcester and Swindon were then home until a move to Gloucester (Horton Road) in June 1956. This was its home shed when seen here, on 23 August 1958, but a move to deepest south west Wales came in November 1960, to Neyland, from where withdrawal came after just nine months. Interestingly, the Bachmann OO model of a BR '45XX' 2-6-2T Small Prairie Tank Loco is this engine, complete with early BR 'lion and wheel' emblem and 'weathered', echoing the condition seen here!

These days the bay is No 3 and no longer serves the erstwhile Ledbury branch, passenger services having been withdrawn from there on 13 July 1959. In this view on 11 July 2007 – almost exactly 48 years on – the cab of the approaching unit is roughly where the tank stood. No 158819, in Arriva grey livery, arrives at the station – 'Central' was dropped from the name in May 1968 – as 2G58, the Arriva Wales 1117 Maesteg-Gloucester 'stopper'. This more head-on view has been chosen as, otherwise, there would have merely been a view of the side of the unit – not particularly inspiring! *Gerald Adams, MJS collection/MJS*

GLOUCESTER CENTRAL: On 7 April 1962 members of the Leicester Railway History Society visited Gloucester and were royally treated. One of their number here captures a quiet moment at Central, looking eastwards along Platform 2, with the bay platform to the right. A guard's van brings up the rear of a freight on the up though road. Note the water column, covered footbridge and the ornate station buildings behind the up platform. Within six years the trackwork was re-organised, with the installation of turnouts complicating this simple arrangement. The suffix 'Central' was added from 17 September 1951, to distinguish it from its ex-MR/LMS neighbour, but, as already mentioned, this only last for 17 years – a somewhat perverse decision, as the Eastgate facility was then still open!

In this overcast view from 15 September 2006, comparatively little has changed over the intervening 44 years, but there are differences. This western end of the 1914 up platform, to the left in this view, has been graced with glazing, presumably to protect waiting passengers from wind and rain after this former parcels platform was re-opened to passenger use in 1984. However, as most trains actually stop closer to the distant footbridge, it would seem to be of little practical use. Note that the covered footbridge has gone – demolished in the 1960s. A new colour light signal gantry has been erected and the trackwork again altered to revert to closer to the original design. Finally, the up canopy now looks a little naked, devoid as it is of the previous attractively designed buildings. *Barry Hilton/MJS*

GLOUCESTER CENTRAL: Following closure of Eastgate on 1 December 1975, Central was redeveloped at a cost of £1½ million, to handle all traffic into the city. Part of this involved the further lengthening of Platform 2, opened by the Mayor of Gloucester on 8 March 1977 – ironically (or was it by design?) the new platform length was 1,977 feet! Now one of the longest in the country, it was subdivided into No 2 at the western end and No 1 at the eastern end, with the former No 1 – the western bay – becoming No 3. In distinctly inclement weather, on 3 November 1979, No 45125 draws to a halt in Platform 2 with a Cardiff-Newcastle train. The old station buildings on this side were swept away in the 1977 redevelopment, replaced by this rather featureless rectangular structure. No 45125 lasted until withdrawal from Tinsley depot on 7 May 1987.

Thirty years on, most is readily identifiable, but there have been changes – in addition to the weather! The new footbridge – obviously installed before the Disability Discrimination Act! – commands the view, but more subtle changes are the arrival of the Pumpkin café, a large advertising hoarding and the explosion of greenery, on and off the platform. On 11 July 2007 No 143603 waits to begin its relatively short journey as 2B82, the First Great Western 1202 service to Swindon. *Tom Heavyside/MJS*

GLOUCESTER CENTRAL: In steam days it was common for there to be a station pilot loco, ready to help out with failures or more menial tasks. Watching these engines – often tanks – bustling to and fro around the station complex was a delight for thousands of spotters as they awaited the next train arrival. On 22 August 1964 this photographer, looking eastwards from Platform 2, has captured No 4107 indulging in a little push-pull carriage shunting. A long-time resident of Tyseley shed, on the southern outskirts of Birmingham, South Wales beckoned in November 1952 before a two-year sojourn in Cornwall, then back to the Principality. When seen here, No 4107 was an incumbent of Cardiff (Canton) and it is interesting to speculate why it is on station pilot duties in Gloucester! The end came, at Severn Tunnel Junction, on 13 June 1965. Note the full gasholder in the distance. *R. E. Toop*

15

GLOUCESTER CENTRAL: Having snapped No 45125 arriving at Gloucester on 3 November 1979 – see page 14 – our photographer has moved east along the platform extension and now captures the Cardiff-Newcastle train snaking past what is now Platform 1. To the right the sidings still hold freight traffic, with, beyond, the tall British Telecom building.

Again the weather is in stark contrast to the earlier view, as is the equivalent service, seen on 11 July 2007. No 170104 runs through Platform 1 before halting outside the station buildings on Platform 2 to form 1V14, the Central Trains 0900 Nottingham-Cardiff Central semi-fast service. Elsewhere everything is as before, with the exception of the extreme right, where Cotswold Rail has taken residence on the former sidings, and the huge building has disappeared. Nos 31452 and 45112 *Royal Army Ordnance Corps* stand with some of Cotswold's coaching stock. *Tom Heavyside/MJS*

16

GLOUCESTER CENTRAL: Further along the 1,977-foot platform, and earlier in time on 18 October 1971, D1748 uses the down through road to haul its rake of coal hoppers away from South Wales. Seen here in the pre-TOPS era, Brush-built D1748, new in July 1964, was to become 47155 in February 1974, 47660 on 18 December 1986 and finally 47815 on 31 August 1989, as BR made refinements to its original design. Initially a Western Region engine, it moved to the Midland Region in October 1967 and thence to the Eastern in November 1972, after which it was a much-travelled loco and by 2007 was still in operation, with Riviera Trains. Its livery here – though barely noticeable! – is original two-tone green but with full yellow ends; ironically, at the time of writing it is back in this livery (but with just a lower yellow warning panel) after a multitude of previous coats! Note the attractive goods shed on the right, and the approach to the still extant Eastgate station on the left.

Following the re-opening of the up platform in 1984, up and down traffic kept much closer to its own side of the station, but with roads becoming bi-directional in case of need. Thus on 11 July 2007 an empty steel train bound for Margam in South Wales disappears past the long down platform. Greenery and landscaping for a new road now disguise the previous entry to Eastgate station, lighting has been updated, the goods shed has been replaced by a warehouse for Pickfords Removals, and Cotswold Rail occupies the previous sidings, with the fronts of Nos 31452 and 33202 visible among the coaches. *Tom Heavyside/MJS*

GLOUCESTER CENTRAL: Finally we reach the end of the long platform! Turning through 180° from previous views and looking east, we see another view now almost extinct but which was wholly unremarkable at the time. No 47511 *Thames*, in BR blue, approaches and makes for Platform 2 with a Plymouth-Manchester Piccadilly cross-country service on 20 October 1982. To continue its journey, No 47511 will have to run round its train and exit the station on this same line before swinging northwards onto the Bristol-Birmingham main line. It is this need for reversal that has caused Virgin Trains to boycott the Gloucester stop and the authorities to think of re-siting the station closer to the north-south line, albeit further away from the city centre. Later to become No 47714 – and named *Grampian Region* between May 1985 and February 1989 – 2007 saw the loco owned by Cotswold Rail and based at Norwich Crown Point depot. The remains of Horton Road engine shed can be seen on the left, while on the right the landscaping of the old approach to Eastgate station is taking shape.

Only detail differences are visible 25 years later, apart from the length and type of cross-country passenger stock. The engine shed yard on the left has largely been abandoned; bushes now screen the new road on the right; the turnout between the two tracks has been smoothed and the pointwork moved closer to the platform; ground signals have appeared; and there are subtle changes in the gantry furniture. On 11 July 2007 twin '170' sets, with No 170116 closest to the camera, leave with 1M62, the Central Trains 1045 Cardiff Central-Nottingham service. Note the large 'X' patch in the unit window, the reason for which is obscure. *Tom Heavyside/MJS*

GLOUCESTER CENTRAL: On 6 April 1963 No 1472 stands in the erstwhile Platform 6, with sidings and goods warehousing beyond. Often used for push-pull duties, it would be interesting to know the precise job being done here, as the engine bears a lamp code for a pick-up freight! New in April 1936 as No 4872 at Danygraig shed in South Wales, it quickly moved to Carmarthen, where it stayed until 25 February 1956, having been renumbered 1472 on 2 November 1946. A 2½-year stay at Newton Abbot preceded five months at Weymouth before reallocations to Cheltenham, then Gloucester. Withdrawn from Horton Road shed on 9 November 1964, it was sold on to Cashmore's yard in Newport for scrap, having run close to 600,000 miles in its 28-year life. Another locomotive favoured as a model, No 1472 was introduced to Dapol's 'N' gauge range in post-war GWR green livery.

The tracks adjacent to the old Platform 6 have long since been ripped up, leaving behind an area for nature and occasional parking! On 11 July 2007 the comparative view shows preserved 'Peak' No 45112 *Royal Army Ordnance Corps*, now under the care of Cotswold Rail. Built at Crewe Works in March 1962, it is seen here in the BR blue livery it wore for so long after renumbering in August 1973. New to Derby shed, it spent its first decade there and at Cricklewood and Nottingham before finally ending up on the Eastern Region, at Tinsley, from where it was withdrawn on 7 May 1987. Happily, preservation beckoned and it was formally reinstated to the serving register on 26 May 1999. Pickfords Removals warehouse is again seen in the background. *Gerald Adams, MJS collection/MJS*

GLOUCESTER CENTRAL: Swinging through 90°, on 6 April 1963, No 6137 is seen arriving at Platform 2 with a three-coach local – probably from Bristol. Note the large structure on the right, housing the Central end of a 250-yard-long covered walkway to Eastgate station. Taken on a late spring afternoon, there is a soporific air about the scene. Having spent much of its life hauling commuters into and out of Paddington, No 6137 moved west to Bristol (Bath Road) shed in July 1955, before turning north, to Gloucester (Horton Road), on 4 October 1958, its allocation when seen here. Another move came five months after this view, to Tyseley, before ending up at Stourbridge Junction shed – possibly for the shuttle service to Town station – and redundancy on 29 November 1964.

The comparison on 11 July 2007 shows the platform basically unaltered but elsewhere much change. The slightly wider view to the left is deliberate to show No 45112 again, as otherwise there is precious little to whet the aesthetic appetite in the present view. The elongated Platform 2 is seen in its relatively bare glory; trees and bushes hide the road that obliterated the tracks into Eastgate (extreme right); and the water column and semaphore signals have gone, the latter replaced by a new colour light gantry. No 158766 arrives at Platform 4 with 2G12, the First Great Western 1210 Weston-super-Mare to Cheltenham Spa local service. Recently transferred from the north, the unit still bears its previous owner's TransPennine livery. *Gerald Adams, MJS collection/MJS*

GLOUCESTER EASTGATE: More happy memories of bygone days – days of innocence, short trousers, hot summers, cheese and tomato sandwiches and Tizer! On an unidentified date in 1964 a young version of the three witches plot at the end of one of Eastgate's platforms, as it tracks approach its ex-GWR neighbour. Whatever they are intent on discussing, they are temporarily oblivious of the hive of activity on Horton Road shed in the distance. This is truly the changeover period, with a diesel present among the steam, and BR Standard 9Fs and ex-LMS 8Fs cheek-by-jowl with ex-GWR locos. The shed closed to steam on 1 January 1966, but continued as a diesel depot of sorts until the 1990s, and now serves as temporary home, without roofed accommodation, for Cotswold Rail locos and other companies' infrastructure machines.

This is not a strict recreation, in view of the disappearance of Eastgate and many other redevelopments over the past 40-plus years, but is a comparative view from the end of Central's current Platform 1 on 11 July 2007. Cotswold Rail's No 47200 *The Fosse Way* and un-numbered 47033 stand outside the newest of the old shed buildings, with No 08936 dumped in the distance, by the roadway. Note the gas holder still in position just visible above the surviving left-hand pitched roof of the original four. This later view shows just how much of the old shed infrastructure has been demolished. *Joe Moss, Roger Carpenter collection/MJS*

TRAMWAY JUNCTION: In this truly delightful scene from 5 September 1948, No 43604 – working for the newly nationalised British Railways, but still wearing its 'LMS 3604' persona – slowly makes its way towards Tramway Junction with a decidedly short freight! It is approaching the bottleneck crossing of Horton Road from the throat of lines from Eastgate station. Allocated to the ex-LMS shed at Gloucester (Barnwood) when seen here, it was soon despatched north to Sheffield (Grimethorpe) shed, where it stayed until withdrawal on 2 January 1954.

Today's comparison is bare, to put it mildly, and is difficult to accurately recreate, as the entrance to Eastgate on the left has been totally subsumed beneath a new road, the view of which is shielded by the growth of trees and bushes. Once again, the abandonment of the former shed yard at Horton Road on the right is plain to see on 11 July 2007, but at least the two distant churches are now more prominent. *P. M. Alexander, Roger Carpenter collection/MJS*

TRAMWAY JUNCTION: Facing east on 16 September 1975, double-headed Nos 20157 and 20172 pass Barnwood from the Cheltenham direction and head for South Wales with a mixed freight of vans and open wagons. Emerging from English Electric's Vulcan Foundry within two months of each other, between 2 September and 28 October 1966, both locos were originally allocated to the Nottingham District, to handle coal and other goods traffic around Toton and the East Midlands generally. With the influx of new-style heavy freight locomotives throughout the 1980s, work for the '20s' became more scarce, on top of the economics of often using them in tandem, and this resulted in their progressive withdrawal. No 20157 was withdrawn from Toton on 10 October 1990, with '172 – which had briefly been renumbered 20305 for six months in 1986 – succumbing the following day.

The road crossing and surroundings remain much as before on the face of it, but there are various detail differences. The footpath now has a raised approach to the crossing, for visually handicapped persons; the crossing barriers are now all white on the skirting and have reflector strips added to the red paint on the beams; the traffic lights have a red and white hatched surround; the turnout between the two closest tracks has been moved further east, away from actually on the crossing itself; there has been some track rationalisation, with the two sidings and buffer stops removed; the prominent point rodding has gone; a 40mph sign and protective barriers have been installed by the tracks; and the roadside fence has been strengthened with a cross beam. On 15 September 2006 No 170631 approaches Gloucester with another Nottingham-Cardiff Central cross-country service. *Tom Heavyside/MJS*

TRAMWAY JUNCTION: This elevated view from the signal box at Tramway Crossing was taken on 7 April 1962, during the photographer's visit to the area with the Leicester Railway History Society, mentioned earlier. Looking back towards the station, the largest of the Horton Road shed buildings is immediately to the right, with an unidentified Class 08 shunter parked alongside. Central to the picture is the gantry controlling movements into and out of Eastgate station, which can just be seen beneath the gantry; the semaphore is raised for the approach of a train to Eastgate. To the left of the gantry and Eastgate signal box, the lime pit is clearly visible alongside the water-softening tower, installed by the Midland Railway for its locos.

Central station is in the mist beyond the right-hand signal gantry. Note the crossing-keeper's shelter in the right foreground; there was a similar facility diagonally across the crossing, on the south side. 'Arthur' and 'Percy' were regulars on the day shifts.

Sadly the signal box has long gone, so we have to view the comparison from ground level. On 11 July 2007 the tracks still make their way to Central station but no longer to Eastgate. Lighting for the road that has swallowed up the former trackbed can be seen towering above the trees and bushes that mark the boundary between it and the railway. *Barry Hilton/MJS*

TRAMWAY JUNCTION: Still in the signal box, but having turned through nearly 180°, we see Tramway Junction in fuller glory. To the left are the lines leading to the northbound Bristol-Birmingham main line, while the tracks in the centre curve away to the south towards Swindon or Bristol. On 7 April 1962 a Class 08 shunter is approaching the station from the nearby sidings, permission being granted by the GWR-pattern semaphore. The area to the right accommodated the BR(W) S&T yard.

By 11 July 2007 the vista has changed! Track has been rationalised and many sidings dispensed with, but the greatest change is the arrival of the flyover road bridge, taking the previously mentioned new road eastwards. The housing seen in the earlier view remains, but is now cut off from view by the road. *Barry Hilton/MJS*

GLOUCESTER SOUTH: The somewhat strangely named 'Gloucester North' signal box (as it would appear to be south rather than north!), seen beyond the 08 on the previous page, is here in closer focus, as viewed from Windmill Parade. Looking towards the Engineer's Depot, light engine No 5206 takes pride of place on 17 August 1962, running towards Tramway Junction and about the emulate the 08's movement seen on page 25. Another of the 1923 variants of Churchward's 2-8-0T design – see page 10 – No 5206 spent virtually the whole of its life in South Wales, with the exception of two months at the end of 1963 at Bristol (St Philips Marsh) shed. Withdrawal came at Pontypool Road shed on 16 May 1966.

The advent of the new road already mentioned totally destroyed chances of a comparative shot, and this is as close as was possible. The Engineer's Depot building still stands, but that is all that is identifiable! The spider's web of sidings has gone, as has the signal box and any other semblance of a railway having been here! This was the view on 15 September 2006. *Ben Ashworth/MJS*

HORTON ROAD SHED – 85B in British Railways' shed codings – was situated by Tramway Crossing, as has been seen. Once boasting a very healthy allocation of no fewer than 101 engines in 1950, it closed to steam on 1 January 1966, but remained open for diesels. However, the vast majority of the old steam shed buildings were razed to the ground. What remained was the least part of the complex – virtually a railway 'lean-to' by now – comprising the former lifting shop and wheel drop. This is seen here on 3 November 1979 with 'Peak' No 45074 standing 'out back' and receiving some attention. Built as D131 at Crewe in December 1961 and allocated to Derby, it remained a Midland loco for the rest of the decade. Renumbered under TOPS to 45074 in January 1975, it travelled widely throughout the UK on various 'mixed traffic' duties – both passenger and freight – before succumbing to the inevitable on 4 September 1985 at Toton depot. Sadly, there was to be no reprieve for this unfortunate, and Vic Berry had cut it up at his Leicester scrapyard site by October 1988.

Gone are the oil drums, fuel tanks and rails and, indeed, any indication of them having been there in the first place, but the building remains, now a listed structure! The old wooden doors have been replaced, superseded by corrugated iron shutters, which, with the discarded gate, Buddleia and other bushes and all manner of detritus, provides a very real air of dereliction on 15 September 2006. Carillion no longer seem to be in residence but their sign prevails. The only sign of life is the tamper just glimpsed in the left distance.
Tom Heavyside/MJS

Left HORTON ROAD SHED: That shed building is seen again here, this time in slightly happier days. On 16 September 1975 Nos 25203 and 25211 stand between duties, with another class member and two 'Peaks'. Initially D7553 and D7561 respectively, they were new within four months of each other in 1965 and were both allocated to the Nottingham District. However, thereafter their fortunes diverged. No 7553 went north to Carlisle Kingmoor depot in October 1967 and was finally withdrawn from Cricklewood in December 1980, whereas '61 headed south for London in April of that year and lasted longer, surviving until 25 July 1986, at Crewe Diesel Depot. The former was cut up at Swindon Works in February 1982, while No 25211's last working was on 14 June 1986, hauling a failed No 37509 and its train – 1J18, the 0725 Birmingham-Aberystwyth – from Caersws to Machynlleth, where it was terminated.

On 11 July 2007 there are still locos present, but the complement is much reduced. From left to right, Nos 47200 *The Fosse Way*, 47033 (painted but un-numbered) and 08936 (in a now faded but still unusual livery of orange and grey) stand forlorn and to some extent abandoned. Note the evidence of the infilling in the previous pits, between the rails in front of the 08 and on the adjacent track, together with the more open vista since the removal of the large British Telecom building. No 08936 was originally withdrawn, from March depot, on 11 December 1992, but was rescued from store and reinstated on 26 October 2001. *Tom Heavyside/MJS*

HORTON ROAD SHED: At the shed in happier times, No 2219 rests outside the substantial 1854 brick-built, single-gable-roofed four-road shed on 6 October 1951, a visitor from Machynlleth. A long-term resident of that mid-Wales shed – note the 89C shedplate on the smokebox – it moved to Oswestry in November 1953, Newport (Ebbw Junction) in October 1959 and, finally, Taunton on 18 June 1960. Withdrawal was on 13 April 1964. Judging from the condition of parts of the loco it looks to have received some attention, but, judging by the 'British Railways' legend still on the tender – three years into Nationalisation – it is not on its way back from Swindon Works. Horton Road resident No 4059 *Princess Patricia*, on the left, awaits her next turn, but not for much longer, as the end came for her on 6 September 1952. *MJS collection*

HORTON ROAD SHED: These two further views of the shed in steam days date from 23 June 1963. Fired up and raring to go, a presentably clean No 7034 *Ince Castle* stands alongside No 5914 *Ripon Hall*, outside that same 1854 building on a very blustery day. The position of the lamp on the 'Castle' seems to indicate an 'ordinary passenger, branch passenger or "mixed" train', an indication of how top-link duties were beginning to be taken over by diesels in ever greater numbers at this time, relegating the steam to more mundane chores; indeed, in earlier times these later-built 'Castles' were not allocated to Gloucester. New as late as 31 August 1950, No 7034 came here in December 1961, reduced to second-string duties after top jobs at Bristol. Withdrawal was on 11 July 1965, close to the end of steam on the Western Region of BR.

Out in the yard, a distinctly non-GWR loco stands by the shed's turntable. No 90040, ex-WD 77430 and 1946 LNER 3040, was built by the North British Locomotive Co in 1944. Allocated to Woodford Halse shed on the ex-GCR main line when seen here, it moved to Nottingham six months later in December 1963, back to Woodford Halse for just seven days in April 1964, then to its last home, Rose Grove, in the North West, from where it was dispensed with on 11 September 1965. It was presumably at Gloucester having worked an inter-regional freight turn. *Both MJS*

GLOUCESTER EASTGATE: Compare this view with that on page 21. On 3 July 1963 more spotters populate the platform seen on that earlier page, on the extreme right here, no doubt appreciating the view of No 92247 on the left as it prepares to pass Horton Road shed with an up freight. The view from this platform, however, is dominated by 'Gloucester Passenger Stn' signal box, with its hoard of coal stashed away under the access stairs, ready for the signalman's stove! Note that the gasholder is still full.

In the second view of the signal box it is slightly obscured by the lamp standard and signal gantry. With the long shadows of evening falling upon the platform, No 7023 *Penrice Castle* has the road to continue its journey to Wolverhampton (Low Level) on 29 August 1964. Another of the class new in British Railways days, No 7023 appeared in July 1949, going first to Cardiff (Canton) shed. This was its only home until 13 August 1960, when it moved north-east to Worcester. A further move, north to Oxley on 20 June 1964, was its last, so that on withdrawal in February 1965 it had served just three sheds in its 15-year career. *A. W. V. Mace collection, Roger Carpenter collection/Gerald Adams collection, MJS collection*

Ledbury branch

BARBERS BRIDGE: Travelling west from Central station, the railway crosses the River Severn twice (counting the East Channel) and, in steam days, immediately after the second crossing the Ledbury branch swung north-west from the South Wales line at Over Junction. The first station on the branch, not far short of 4 miles from the junction, was Barbers Bridge. Opened on 27 July 1885, together with the rest of the branch, it was somewhat strangely named as there is no place of that name. Situated adjacent to the B4215, its nearest place of any size was Tibberton, some three-quarters of a mile to the west. On a single-track stretch, as seen here, traffic was never heavy and, despite railcars introduced from 1940, passenger facilities were withdrawn on 13 July 1959. Freight traffic – only as far as Dymock by that time – ceased on 1 June 1964 and the track past Barbers Bridge was lifted within two weeks! As seen on 10 July 1959 – just three days before closure – the station master's house stands on the right and looks to have been remodelled since originally built. Note the large canopy, three highly ornate chimneys and a short siding just beyond the platform.

Since closure, the B4215 has been realigned, severing the trackbed immediately south of the station site and leaving the former road overbridge isolated. This is the comparative view, from that bridge, on 2 August 2006, from which can be seen that the station master's house has been the recipient of further development and extension. The centre depression betrays the course of the trackbed and the station building is still extant beyond the far hedgerow. Surrounding trees have grown substantially over the years! *R. M. Casserley/MJS*

BARBERS BRIDGE: At ground level, this is the view back to the road bridge. There is but one person on the platform, but whether she is a friend of the photographer or waiting for the diesel railcar that is just visible through the bridge – the 6.25pm service from Gloucester – is unknown. The date is also unknown, but, judging from other views that have been seen, it is almost certainly in the very last days of the branch passenger service. Parcel trolleys wait hopefully on the platform and the corrugated iron store will probably not see much more use.

The date of the second view is 11 July 1959 and No 3203 restarts its train from the platform with the last passenger train over the branch, to the accompaniment of waves, raised hats, people watching from the bridge and heads peering out from the carriage windows. What a shame that the throng on the platform and on the train – warranting five coaches! – could not have been an everyday occurrence. A long-term servant of the West Midlands and north-east Wales, No 3203 drifted south to Gloucester (Horton Road) shed on 1 November 1952, from where it was withdrawn on 28 December 1963. *P. J. Garland, Roger Carpenter collection/Hugh Ballantyne*

BARBERS BRIDGE: It is now nine years from withdrawal of passenger services and four since closure of this stretch of the branch. However, apart from the removal of the rails and the growth of flowers and grass, relatively little appears to have changed on 24 July 1968. There is fencing now separating the station building and station master's house from the trackbed, and presumably these two properties are now in private hands; the latter is still in the same state as when seen in 1959. Other visitors survey the scene from the road bridge.

With a hedge now separating the two properties and preventing a meaningful comparative shot, this is the eastward view of the old trackbed and station master's house on 2 August 2006. Note that the latter has been extended at the far end, doubling its profile to the railway/garden. The previous trackbed has been severed, as previously stated, by a realignment of the B4215, just a few yards beyond the bridge, but a view of this is impeded by growth of bushes over recent years.

Turning through 180°, this is the delightful view of the station platform and former trackbed. It is pleasing to see both the retention of the fretted awning and the tasteful way in which the previous 'wilderness' has been transformed into a most attractive garden. Tasteful and sympathetic are words that come to mind! *Robin Leleux/MJS, with permission (2)*

MALSWICK HALT: During 1937/38 the GWR opened three halts on the Ledbury branch, in an attempt to encourage traffic. Malswick Halt opened on 1 January 1938, but the trial was not successful, leading to the cessation of passenger services on the branch on 11 July 1959, as already noted. This is a view of the station 'approach' eight days after this. Notice the less than inviting entrance to the station, with tall grass, deteriorating sign and rickety steps – no attempt to provide for disabled travellers here! The Birmingham-registered Rover looks a little out of place in these surroundings!

With the hedge and the neatly trimmed mini-embankment totally disguising the previous entrance, we are left to confirm the location by the extant bridge parapets, covered as they are with more than 40 years of unfettered growth. As seen on 2 August 2006, the sleek BMW with the personalised numberplate maintains the standard of road vehicle!

Having negotiated the steps, this was the view at rail level, towards Ledbury, on the same day as the top view, 19 July 1959. Apart from the disconnection of the gas lamp, the halt looks in fine condition and the track has obviously seen some recent re-sleepering and ballasting – typical when the branch was about to be downgraded! *P. J. Garland, Roger Carpenter collection (2)/MJS*

NEWENT: Continuing with views by this photographer on his visit to the branch on 19 July 1959, we have now reached Newent. Situated on a brief east-west stretch of the line, approached from the B4215 road at the northern edge of the town, the station had two platforms set on either side of an 800-foot loop, and was the most important station on the branch so far, befitting the size of its catchment area. Looking back towards Gloucester, the tidy appearance gives no indication that passenger services have already ended, with seats, station gardens and parcel barrows awaiting the next load!

A look at the same place on 2 August 2006 is not so attractive. Fenced off and without access, this was the nearest comparison that could be had on this day. Much of the 300-foot up platform remains, but the down one has disappeared, as has the bridge over the B4215, in the right distance. Elsewhere all manner of detritus has been dumped on the site, leading to a very depressing scene! *P. J. Garland, Roger Carpenter collection/MJS*

NEWENT: An undated view but a delightful one! Judging by the fashions, this looks to be mid-to-late-1950s and quite conceivably a Saturday, with groups of locals possibly travelling to Gloucester for a bout of shopping. The original design of GWR diesel railcars, first introduced in 1934, featured 'air-smoothed' bodywork, which was very much the fashion at the time. The rounded lines of the first examples built led to their nickname 'flying banana'; the preserved W4W is an example of the original, rounded body shape and can be seen in Swindon's STEAM Museum. Later examples, such as No 22 (preserved at Didcot), had a much more angular (and practical) bodywork, yet the nickname persisted for these too. This unidentified example – possibly W19W, allocated to Gloucester for some time – is from this later batch, introduced in 1941. Note the platform garden and the generally tidy appearance.

'After the Lord Mayor's Show'! Nine years from the end of passenger turns, and four since total closure, the station site is rapidly being reclaimed by nature. This view from 24 July 1968 shows the main station building still in good shape, and it is a shame that the preservation era had not more fully arrived and, say, the nearby Dean Forest Railway enthusiasts had been around to rescue it for posterity. *MJS collection/Robin Leleux*

NEWENT: For our final look at Newent, we again see No 4573 on its run to Ledbury on 23 August 1958 (see page 12). With the loco available as a model and coaches to accompany, this would make an ideal subject for a modeller to recreate a typical GWR branch-line station! After the end of passenger services on the line, No 4573 went on to give sterling service on the Cheltenham-Kingham route. *Gerald Adams, MJS collection*

FOUR OAKS HALT, 2 miles further on from Newent, was another GWR innovation in 1937, in the attempt to drum up patronage. Opened on 16 October – and built at an estimated cost of just £200! – it sat a quarter of a mile from the hamlet it purported to serve, on the eastern edge of Dymock Wood, reached by a narrow country road. Never likely to generate much revenue, it closed with the other stations on the line in July 1959 to passengers and June 1964 to freight. In this view from 19 July 1959, eight days after the cessation of passenger services, the height of the cutting and the adjacent road bridge can be well judged.

Incredibly this *is* the same location! Infilling is hardly the word to adequately describe the many hundreds of tons of earth that must have been used to fill up the cutting. All that is now left here to signify that there was once a railway through the site is the top layer of the bridge parapet brickwork, just visible among the greenery on 2 August 2006. *P. J. Garland, Roger Carpenter collection/MJS*

FOUR OAKS HALT: Two-and-a-half years later, the view from that road bridge captures No 2232 making its leisurely way back to Gloucester on 24 January 1962. The gas lamp holder remains, but without attachments; the platform fencing and waiting shelter have both gone; and the once-fenced pathway down to the platform is still just visible in the lower left quadrant. In the distance, a new addition at the time was the bridge carrying the M50 motorway over the railway. Not officially allocated to Gloucester until three days after this view, No 2232 has obviously arrived early and been put to immediate use. Earlier homes had been Croes Newydd, Stourbridge Junction, Shrewsbury, Machynlleth, and Bristol (St Philips Marsh). The stay at Gloucester lasted until 6 April 1963, when the loco moved to Worcester, from where the end came on 12 October 1964.

Again, the view on 2 August 2006 bears little resemblance to that of 40-plus years earlier. Only the trees on either side of the erstwhile railway remain, now much larger and in leaf, together with the M50 bridge, still carrying traffic over the site. At least the trackbed under that bridge has not been totally obliterated! Tarmac Construction built the 21-mile-long motorway, sometimes colloquially known as the Ross Spur, between 1958 and 1962, with this section opened in 1960. Being part of a strategic route from the Midlands to South Wales, it was constructed as an early priority and is one of the few British motorways not to have been widened, retaining its original layout of only two lanes in each direction. *Ben Ashworth/MJS*

DYMOCK: A little short of 2 miles almost due north of Four Oaks, Dymock was a more substantial station, befitting the larger place it served, situated on the junction of the B4216 to Ledbury and B4215 'Roman Road' towards Leominster. Opened in July 1885, it boasted a loop, with two platforms and a delightful station building on the up (north-eastern) side. At its height it enjoyed a full range of both passenger and freight facilities and had the use of a goods shed and 5-ton crane. There was no footbridge access to the down platform (to the left in this view) and passengers had to reach this by the barrow crossing at the southern end of the platforms; no doubt the boarded crossing seen here, mid-way along the platforms, was for staff only! Presenting a delightful portrait of a GWR wayside station some time around the mid-1950s, an unidentified '45XX' 2-6-2T arrives with a Ledbury-Gloucester local. Three staff members await the arrival and a parcels trolley has bags awaiting attention. Note the well-kept gardens on both sides.

Seen from the same vantage point on 2 August 2006, the down platform is still in situ, complete with edging stones, forming an easy pathway for occupants of the retirement home built on the site of the former up-side station buildings (right). The road bridge, too, remains and the right-hand abutment can just be seen between the two clipped bushes in the centre of the picture. The former trackbed between the platforms has been infilled as far as the bushes. The down waiting shelter, on the extreme left in line with the boarded crossing, was removed after closure and now graces the platform at Norchard (Low Level) on the Dean Forest Railway. *MJS collection/MJS*

DYMOCK: Looking towards Gloucester in the spring of 1959, this is the view of the station around three months before the end for passengers. The topiary and generally well-kept gardens, tidy platforms, seat and trolleys all paint a healthy picture, somewhat let down by the up track looking as if it could benefit from the weedkilling train. The goods shed can just be seen beyond the end of the up platform, with a box van standing outside, and the signal box is on the bend, on the down side. Just one car waits in the car park.

Moving forward nine years, the scene is so very different. On 24 July 1968 the fir tree remains, as does the up station building, now contained behind fencing, and the goods shed, though now without tracks or traffic. Elsewhere, the telegraph pole on the down platform fights a rearguard action against Mother Nature and the platforms are still defiant, but the sense of dereliction is almost painful.

The view on 2 August 2006 is both more open and more enclosed! The retirement home mentioned previously can just be glimpsed beyond the three cars in a line. Happily, the platform faces are both still extant at this northern end, with the old trackbed not filled in to quite the same extent as on the previous page. The fir trees have gone, but those on the down platform have been allowed to flourish, now hiding the earlier views. Perhaps one should be grateful for small mercies, that evidence of the old station has not been totally disguised. *Joe Moss, Roger Carpenter collection/Robin Leleux/MJS*

DYMOCK: A final view of the train hauled by No 4573 on 23 August 1958, previously seen at Gloucester and Newent. Here it pauses at Dymock, but while the sight of the loco and its train enlivens the view, there is a distinct lack of human presence! Evidence of some future traffic is betrayed by the milk churns just visible on the up platform on the left. The very clean lines of the '45XX' make for a very attractive portrait. The substantial canopy on this platform was unusual in having some glazing, allowing a greater volume of light onto the waiting passengers than would otherwise be the case. *Gerald Adams, MJS collection*

GREENWAY HALT: Another of the latterday halts – opened on 1 April 1937 – this minimalist station was set in open countryside, as can be seen in this view from 21 March 1959. Less than a mile from Dymock, Greenway Halt was the last station on this route in Gloucestershire and was around a quarter of a mile from the hamlet it served and the same distance further to Donnington Hall, both situated on the other side of the River Leadon from the station. Closure came with the rest of the route, so W19W, seen here on its way to Ledbury forming the 4.08pm local from Gloucester, is less than four months from the end. Note that the gas lamp has gone and the poster, presumably announcing the end of passenger services, is already peeling from its board.

Sheep may safely graze, and so may horses. The very open nature of the area is yet more obvious from this view

on 2 August 2006, and infilling of the former shallow cutting has attempted to obliterate evidence of the railway, but the course of the old line is still plainly visible, despite the deposits of animal waste and tractor tracks at this end! *John Spencer Gilks/MJS*

Gloucester Eastgate and ex-LMS lines to the north

GLOUCESTER EASTGATE: Though physically sited just to the south of Central, Eastgate was the departure point for MR/LMS trains for the north. Closed in 1975, it is now mourned locally and, judging by the number of cars in the station forecourt on 24 July 1968, would appear to have been popular even then and another decision based on politics, rather than traffic figures! Developed on a sharp curve from the joint throat with the GWR at Tramway Crossing, it gave both a through route to Bristol from the north without reversal and to the docks area by the Gloucester & Berkeley Canal. The imposing entrance to the station, dating from 1896, is well seen in this view.

Following closure the entire site was razed to the ground over the next two years and redeveloped. The layout is now totally subsumed beneath an Asda supermarket and one half of the newly created Bruton Way dual-carriageway. This is the view on 15 September 2006 across that new road, plainly demonstrating how completely the previous layout has been lost. The supermarket is the white building through the trees, only roughly approximating to the axis of the old station. *Robin Leleux/MJS*

Right GLOUCESTER EASTGATE: Inside the station the curvature of the platforms is clear, as is the substantial but rather plain architecture bequeathed by the Midland Railway. Waiting travellers prepare to board as D106 arrives with the northbound 1N68, the 4.45pm Bristol (Temple Meads)-Bradford (Forster Square) cross-country service, on Good Friday, 20 April 1962. New on 17 June the previous year and bearing the 17A shedplate of its first allocation, the 'Peak' became No 45106 under TOPS – almost the only Class 45 to have a number bearing any relevance to its earlier one, as members of the class were numbered in apparently random fashion. Having been a Midland Region engine for the first decade of its life, it finally ended up an Eastern incumbent, joining the vast majority of its siblings at Tinsley Depot. Unofficially named *Vulcan* on 18 August 1987 at Tinsley, withdrawal came on 27 July 1988. Reinstated just seven days later, this new lease of life was to be short-lived, the end coming on 20 February 1989. Initially stored at Woodhouse Junction, the cutter's torch was applied at C. F. Booth's Rotherham scrapyard in April 1992. *Michael Mensing*

This page GLOUCESTER EASTGATE: This is the view from the southern end of station. On 16 September 1975, less than three months from the end, No 25152 heads north-east with a rake of empty coal hoppers. Note the delightful Barton Street Junction signal box next to the level crossing, overseeing the traffic passing under it. New as D7502 in October 1964 and initially allocated to Nottingham, it became 25152 in April 1974 under the TOPS system renumbering, by which time it had had six changes of allocation and had temporarily ended up in the North West, around Liverpool. Withdrawn from Cricklewood in January 1984, it was sent to BR's Works at Swindon, where it became scrap metal in February 1985.

The comparative view on 15 September 2006 has nothing of immediate resemblance, except for the glimpse of All Saints Church to the left. This side of the dual carriageway occupies the previous trackbed, while the far side is the old road, present but unseen to the right of the 'past' view, on the other side of the fencing. The traffic lights now protect Barton Street (to the left) and Eastgate Street (to the right) from this road, rather than a railway! *Tom Heavyside/MJS*

Below Moving out of the station confines into the bright sunshine of 23 August 1958, 2-6-0 No 42940 accelerates away from the Gloucester stop with a holiday excursion; judging by the 5B Crewe (South) shedplate, it is likely that the train is bound for a destination in the North West. The 'Crab' was a resident of predominantly ex-LNWR sheds for the whole of its BR career, being at Willesden at Nationalisation and working north through the Birmingham area, Crewe, Manchester and the North West before ending up at Stockport (Edgeley). Withdrawal was on 9 October 1965. Note the signal box, already seen, and the low, flat-sided Fowler tender behind the locomotive. *Gerald Adams, MJS collection*

GLOUCESTER EASTGATE: The platform end is again the haunt of spotters on 29 August 1964. In the late afternoon, with shadows creeping along the platform, No 73021 prepares to move forward into the sidings that occupied the ground between the two stations. Meanwhile, an unidentified 'Western' diesel-hydraulic approaches Central station with an express bound for South Wales, and No 48196 is a 'Midland' visitor to the ex-GWR Horton Road shed yard. There is an atmosphere of activity and one can almost feel the anticipation and attention of the spotters! Note the gasholder and shed buildings, seen previously, peering over the view. No 73021 was new in November 1954, going first to Chester shed. A Western Region loco thereafter for its 14-year life, much of its time was spent in or around Wales, but is in the midst of a 14-month stay at Gloucester in this view. Its final home was Oxford, until withdrawal on 19 September 1965 – in steam terms, barely run in! *Gerald Adams, MJS collection*

TRAMWAY JUNCTION: Helped by an appealing light and a sky with character, the judicious use of a telephoto lens here has created a dramatic picture from what would otherwise have been a 'bog standard' shot. At 1.10pm on the afternoon of 17 August 1962 No 44757 heads away from the Eastgate stop with 1E68, the MFO Paignton-Sheffield inter-regional holiday express. The rather pugnacious front appearance of the loco resulted from it being one of the 20 'Black Fives', rebuilt from Stanier's original design by George Ivatt with Caprotti valve gear in 1948, with the outside steam pipes set at an 'aggressive' attitude! Being the last of this development, it also enjoyed other refinements, such as Timken roller bearings and a double chimney. Emerging from Crewe Works in December 1948, it was set to work from Leeds (Holbeck) shed. Its only other homes were Lower Darwen, for 21 days from 9 November 1963, and Southport, until withdrawal on 4 December 1965. *Ben Ashworth*

49

GLOUCESTER BARNWOOD: As Midland Region trains bound for the north left Gloucester and passed over Tramway Junction, they skirted the boundary of Barnwood engine shed. Replacing a roundhouse on the site of what became Eastgate station, Barnwood was opened in 1895. A brick-built affair with three gable-style slated pitched roofs, it later boasted a four-road lifting shop. BR closed it on 4 May 1964, after which all necessary work was done by Horton Road. That day is still some time away here, as No 41535 is captured resting inside the shed in 1959. One of a class designed by Deeley for the Midland Railway in 1907, of which ten survived to be inherited by BR in 1948, No 41535 spent many years at Derby before being moved to Barnwood on 18 May 1957, for use in the nearby docks complex. Here bearing the 'cycling lion', BR's first emblem, it stayed in Gloucester until 28 September 1963 when it moved to South Wales. The end was then not far off, however, coming at Neath shed on 12 October 1964.

There is no proper or meaningful comparative view possible, so this is the view of the Barnwood site from across the tracks on 15 September 2006. The industrial takeover of the site is clear, with Allstone's main building roughly covering the site of the old shed. In the foreground No 60031 *ABP Connect* waits in the loop before negotiating its way through Central station and on to South Wales with a Corby-Margam empty steel train. Note the prolific growth on the ground following the removal of the various sidings. *MJS collection/MJS*

CHURCHDOWN: On 16 August 1964 No 4472 *Flying Scotsman* was a visitor to the former Midland route, at the head of the Warwickshire Railway Society's 'Swindon & Eastleigh Tour'. Seen here at approximately 9.50am, there are just a few hardy souls present to witness the scene as the nine-coach southbound train enters Churchdown station. This is actually the second station, opened on 2 February 1874, an incredible 32 years after the first one – which was open for just 49 days in 1842! Initially twin track, the layout was quadrupled in 1942 to cope with extra wartime traffic – the extra tracks can be seen to the left and right in this view. The unimaginative signal box, at the Cheltenham end of the up platform, was opened at the same time. Closure came on 2 November 1964 for both passengers and goods, and the two wartime tracks were removed. Note the platform garden, a feature of the station for many years.

Not far short of three years later, demolition of the station infrastructure is under way in earnest in August 1967. The outer tracks have long gone and the two squat buildings seen on the down platform in the first view are now devoid of roof timbers, doors, etc. The signal box, too, is out of commission. Note the absence of hard hats, high-vis vests and other paraphernalia considered essential in today's Health & Safety-mad regime!

Today there is no evidence of a station ever having been here. On 24 July 2007 the view is so much barer – and the motive power does nothing to lift the spirits to any great degree, despite the vinyl on the bodyside advertising Bristol. With the delightful Gloucestershire countryside stretching out in the distance, No 143621 heads towards its destination at Cheltenham Spa, forming 2G85, the GW 1450 service from Gloucester. *Ben Ashworth (2)/MJS*

CHURCHDOWN: The views on the previous page were from the road overbridge on the outskirts of Churchdown. Moving to the other side of the road, this is the view the other way, looking towards Gloucester. On 27 June 1963 No 42948 heads south with a mixed freight past ex-GWR lower-quadrant semaphore signals. While the GWR and LMS shared the route from Cheltenham to Gloucester, jurisdiction was split and the 2-6-0 is just about the pass the 'Midway Board' into the LMS section. Allocated to Stoke-on-Trent shed at the time, No 42948 was another locomotive that spent the lion's share of its BR life out of ex-LNWR West Coast Main Line sheds.

Once more, the removal of the 1942 tracks – and here, too, the semaphore signals – has led to a much reduced level of interest, while the prolific growth of trees and bushes has created a green canopy that disguises what was once so visible in the 'past' view. On 24 July 2007 the rather unimaginatively named HST power car No 43009 *First – Transforming Travel* brings up the rear of 1L67, the GW 1446 Cheltenham Spa-London Paddington service. On the right puddles remain from the heavy rains of Friday 20 July that contributed to such flooding devastation in Gloucestershire. *Ben Ashworth/MJS*

LANSDOWN JUNCTION: Some 2½ miles north of Churchdown and still in the 'joint' GWR/LMS section, Lansdown Junction was the parting of the ways for the branch to Andoversford and beyond as it left Cheltenham. An interesting sight here, looking south on 21 March 1957, is the trial running from Swindon of railcars SC79106 and 79107, negotiating the cat's cradle of tracks at the junction. Designated Class 126 by BR, they were officially released to traffic from Swindon Works the following month and sent to Scotland. Sadly, like so many of the early DMU designs, they did not last overlong, being withdrawn in October 1972 and coming back south to be cut up at Bird's scrapyard at Long Marston in September 1975. Note the rudimentary path on the left leading down to the tracks and the 1942-style signal box, echoing that at Churchdown.

With the withdrawal of passenger services over the former Midland & South Western Junction Railway (M&SWJR) route south of Andoversford, the need for some of the trackwork at Lansdown Junction was removed, and consequently the opportunity was taken to rationalise the layout. This can be judged to some extent in this view of No 7925 *Westol Hall*, approaching the Cheltenham stop with a West of England-Birmingham holiday express on 14 July 1962. The design is now much simpler, without the double diamonds and the multitude of crossovers and pointwork. Note the 108 milepost (the distance from London via the Andoversford branch), the knot of spotters on the footpath, how the foreground shallow embankment has been tidied in the cess, and the growth of trees on the far embankment, hiding from view the buildings seen in 1957. *John Edgington/Edwin Wilmshurst*

LANSDOWN JUNCTION: By 16 September 1975 the trackwork is even simpler, with the branch to Andoversford now completely gone; the former junction is now plain line, and a brick building now sits on the branch trackbed. In the bright late-summer sunshine, No 47105 takes the MR/LMS route for a stop at Cheltenham (Lansdown) station with 1E54, the 0848 Cardiff-Leeds inter-regional service. Appropriately allocated to Cardiff (Canton) depot at the time of this view, it had started life as D1693, emerging from the Brush Works on 6 December 1963. It was a much travelled locomotive, after its first home at Bristol (Bath Road) depot, with withdrawal coming early in 1994. Happily, it survived to be bought privately and now resides on the Gloucestershire Warwickshire Railway, not far from this location.

It is not now possible to obtain the clear views seen earlier, this private covered walkway spoiling the view. It

was built when the former GWR tracks were still in situ, as evidenced by the smoke shields on the underside, but those tracks have been absent for some time, with the result that the layout around the junction has been further simplified. A siding still remains in the distance on 28 June 2006, but otherwise it is all plain line, utilising the former LMS route into Cheltenham. *Tom Heavyside/ MJS*

CHELTENHAM: Stepping across the main A40 road into the town, with Lansdown Junction now behind us, the separation of the old adversaries' tracks at this point is clear. To the right, the former GWR route to St James station heads straight for the centre of the town, whereas on the left the ex-Midland route swings north and bisects the more western fringes. On 21 March 1957 ex-GWR No 2891 runs light engine on the up (northbound) Midland track, as a train waits for the road in the down platform of Lansdown station. Note the wonderful array of semaphore signals.

Oh, how times change! Instantly recognisable as the same location, the view on 28 June 2006 is vastly poorer in interest. Gone are the semaphores, the up Midland siding and the ex-GWR tracks, a Post Office building has been built across the GWR's trackbed, and extensions have been made to the Midland platforms. There are constant calls for the Gloucestershire Warwickshire Railway to be allowed to extend south into Cheltenham proper, and possibly even regain through running to this point, as, remarkably, access is still possible, but whether these will ever be satisfied is open to question. No 170109, in the later Central Trains blue and grey livery, approaches Lansdown station as 1M62, the 1045 Cardiff Central-Nottingham cross-country service. *John Edgington/MJS*

CHELTENHAM LANSDOWN: This close-up of Lansdown station shows it in very much its original state, with short platforms for such a main-line facility, which occasionally meant trains of any length having to stop twice! On 6

May 1956 No 40454 has arrived from Nottingham Midland with the RCTS (East Midlands Branch) 'East Midlander No 2 Railtour', and is standing at the end of the down (southbound) platform; it will shortly be joined by 'sister' No 40489, to continue the journey to Swindon Works by way of Andoversford and the M&SWJR. The third (bay) platform face, to the right of the train, was added in 1891 in conjunction with the opening of that route from Swindon Town station, but this short addition to the station was often also used in connection with traffic to the local racecourse and/or the famed girls school. Note, to the right, beyond the right-hand signal gantry and loading gauge, the impressive Doric colonnade entrance to the station; however, impressive as it was, it was sadly removed in 1961. Note also the predominance of suits and ties of the tour members!

Nearly two decades later there have been changes. The GWR tracks still survive (bottom right), but Lansdown's bay platform has gone, as has the pitched roof to this end of the canopy on the down platform. The level of the site of the bay platform has been lowered and cars are starting to encroach. The previous boundary between station forecourt and bay platform and sidings is marked by the three tall trees by the cars. On 16 September 1975 D1048 *Western Lady* rounds the sharp curve with a rake of southbound china clay empties. New from Crewe Works on 15 December 1962, to Cardiff (Canton), it was withdrawn from service on 28 February 1977, but escaped scrapping to be preserved by the Midland Diesel Group at Butterley. At the time of writing it is receiving attention to bodywork and electrical installations. *MJS collection/Tom Heavyside*

CHELTENHAM LANSDOWN: Stripped of its Doric colonnade, the station entrance, as seen by those approaching from the town, here looks bare and vaguely embarrassed at its nakedness! On 24 July 1968, seven years after removal of the main structure, one column survives on the left, though damaged at the top, and the front of the building still bears the scars of the surgery. Period cars await their owners; the centre poster announces Car Park tariffs; cars now park on the left where once there was a small garden area; and the centre chimney seems to have been rebuilt, previously having matched its neighbour to the left.

Happily, by 28 June 2006 common sense (and an appreciation of customer perception) has prevailed. Once more graced with cover for travellers emerging from the building and perhaps waiting for cars to meet them, the frontage has been re-rendered and repainted. The left-hand column has been tidied, a doorway has been converted to a window, fresh lighting has been installed, together with two telephone kiosks, the car park has again been remodelled, and the station is now proud to announce who it is! There are even window boxes on the first floor waiting to be filled, but note the total absence of chimneys. *Robin Leleux/MJS*

CHELTENHAM LANSDOWN: A lorry leaves the town across the A40 bridge in the distance as No 47656 leaves Lansdown station with the 0918 Manchester Piccadilly-Plymouth inter-regional express on 18 March 1989. The bare branches in the foreground belong to one of the three trees seen previously, marking the extent of the bay platform and sidings. The number of cars is expanding, necessitating this 'overflow' car park. The course of the ex-GWR tracks to St James station runs along the wall in the left background. Subsequently renumbered 47811 4½ months later, on 4 August, the Class 47 was still active in 2007 as a member of Freightliner's fleet.

Such has been the explosion in car use, even in the short 17 years since the 'past' view, that the car park is now full and has had white markings painted in an attempt to more closely control where cars are parked. New platform fencing and lighting has been installed and the First Great Western HST set provides the modern equivalent of the previous express. Note the arrival of the Royal Mail building now occupying part of the old trackbed. Also noticeable is the increase in the size of the cars! *Both MJS*

CHELTENHAM LANSDOWN: This undated view from around 1962/3 was taken from Platform 1, looking north towards Birmingham, complete with water column for thirsty steam engines. Note the short up platform and the open bay platform on the left, and the two inter-platform bridges, one with buildings spanning the tracks.

Five years later, on 24 July 1968, relatively little has changed, with the exception of the removal of the water column and the extension of the up Platform 2, completed in 1965 – note the altered brickwork for this extension below platform level. Platform lighting has also been updated on the right. A two-car DMU has just arrived from Swindon.

Into the 21st century, much remains the same. Now known merely as Cheltenham Spa, having lost the 'Lansdown' suffix, the columns and fine tracery supports for the station's roof survive, but the pitched glazing of the latter has now gone, although the replacement still does not seem to shed much more light onto waiting passengers! On 28 June 2006 No 43190, forming a service from Paddington, pauses for its passengers to alight before moving into a siding to the north of the station. To the right, a Nottingham-Cardiff semi-fast draws into Platform 1. Note the addition of non-slip paving along the length of the platform. *Bob Essery, Roger Carpenter collection/Robin Leleux/ MJS*

CHELTENHAM LANSDOWN: A busy time at Lansdown! To the left, on 10 April 1995, No 150248 prepares to admit its enthusiastic clutch of passengers before leaving as the 1218 local stopping service to Swindon. In Platform 2, to the right, No 158860 is of more modern design, as befits its more 'important' duty of handling the 1050 Cardiff Central-Nottingham roster. One wonders how many of these and other travellers notice or appreciate the attractive and delicate tracery on the roof supports!

A decade on and the 'new order' is represented by one of Richard Branson's Virgin 'Voyagers' (the non-tilting variety!), pausing at Cheltenham as 1V41, the 1112 Birmingham New Street-Plymouth train. Sleek and attractive in its red and grey coat, as seen on 28 June 2006, this will become 'the past' by the time this book is published, with the announcement of Arriva Trains winning the Cross-Country franchise from November 2007 and proposing to paint the 'Voyagers' in a predominantly grey livery. *Both MJS*

CHELTENHAM LANSDOWN: Moving to Platform 2, the view south finds D86 entering the station at 8.28pm on 7 July 1962 with a decidedly mixed freight. This angle shows the clean lines of the 'Peaks', and, with their low grey body stripe enhancing the attractive green, they were certainly one of the more aesthetically successful diesel designs. New in March 1961 to Derby shed, D86 became 45105 in April 1973 under TOPS. Apart from two months on the WR at Bristol (St Philips Marsh) for crew training, it was exclusively an MR engine for the first decade and spent much time on express duties out of St Pancras, but the 'mixed traffic' nature of the design is here demonstrated. Note the three-way point to the right of the train, giving access from the up siding to the bay, the short stub siding, and onto the main line. Above the body of D86 the cleared signal indicates an expected arrival on the GWR line. *Michael Mensing*

61

CHELTENHAM LANSDOWN: Enhanced by the low camera angle, another 'Peak' is captured at Lansdown from the south, this time on cross-country duties. There were three variants of the original class, becoming Classes 44, 45 and 46 under TOPS. One of the latter type, No 46018 was one of the 57 built with Brush generator and traction motors and was new as D155 in February 1962, again to Derby shed. It was a much-travelled loco from the very start, with 11 moves from the initial allocation in the first six years! Never as successful as their Class 45 brethren, they were withdrawn as a class much earlier, with the first (D142/46005) going in December 1977. The vast majority ended their days at Gateshead, but some finished life many miles from there, at Laira depot in Plymouth. No 46018 was one of these, being put to one side on 14 December 1980, re-instated on 29 November 1981 and finally dispensed with on 18 December 1983. Cutting up was handled at Swindon Works and was completed by 20 April 1985.

As on the Midland Main Line out of St Pancras, the 'Peaks' were displaced on front-line cross-country duties by HSTs during the 1980s. Here No 43123 – one of a handful to have the front end altered by fitment of buffers –

enters Lansdown with the 0720 Penzance-Edinburgh 'Cornish Scot' service on 10 April 1995. Built in April 1979, No 43123 is one of the relatively few of the type never to have been named, and has been a servant of ER depots for the whole of its life. Under the auspices of GNER, it was still very active in 2007. *Tom Heavyside/MJS*

ASHCHURCH was, at its height, both a busy and strategic junction, with branches west to Tewkesbury and Great Malvern and east to Evesham and on to Birmingham. Indeed, although situated on the Midland main line from Birmingham to Bristol, there was even a service to Birmingham from Ashchurch via Evesham – a somewhat circuitous route, via Redditch, that joined up with that main line again at Barnt Green. On 29 July 1961, in the platform on the left No 4614 waits to begin its journey as the 5.10pm branch train to Upton-on-Severn, while D68 restarts from the station stop with the southbound 12.52pm York-Bristol Temple Meads inter-regional express. Dowty's industrial complex – including what had been Bird's custard factory – stands beyond the delightful architecture of Ashchurch station buildings.

What remains of the Dowty Group building, somewhat reduced in stature, is just visible in the distance beyond the 21st-century car park. After the cessation of services to Tewkesbury and Evesham the station was closed and the whole infrastructure here swept away, the platforms as well as the wonderful buildings. Happily, such has been the growth of housing locally and the demands for re-instatement that the station was re-opened, albeit remodelled, on 30 May 1997. All that remains from the past on 2 August 2006, apart from the old Dowty building, are the two main-line tracks, the ex-Evesham branch curving to the right, running into the MoD camp nearby, the substantial water tower at the northern end of the station (seen just above the left-hand end of the footbridge) and the pine tree on the right. *Michael Mensing/MJS*

ASHCHURCH: Three more views of the station from the A46 road bridge. The first is dated 24 July 1968 and another southbound inter-regional train – this time a mixed freight – is seen passing non-stop through the junction station. D1818 roars past the signal box watched by a group of spotters on the left. Trains haven't run from the branch platforms for a few years and track has been lifted; on the left a brick cabin has appeared on the Tewkesbury trackbed. The sharply curving remains of the former Evesham branch can be seen just beyond the utilitarian signal box.

A further seven years have passed and the situation is drastically different. On 15 September 1975 No 46054 accelerates past the site of the station with a very short freight. It is conceivable that the consist is bound for the MoD camp and will negotiate the realigned track to the right. Note the loops on either side of the main line beyond the train.

By 2 August 2006 life has again been breathed into the site. New platforms have appeared, roughly on the site of the originals; the ex-Evesham branch has 'combined' the two views above and now has two tracks (albeit one severed in recent times) to receive the daily train; and a free car park occupies the old Tewkesbury platform and trackbed. The station approach road has been dramatically remodelled following the establishment of an small industrial complex out of the picture to the left. An unidentified Virgin 'Voyager' adds some bright colour to the scene as it speeds north. *Robin Leleux/Tom Heavyside/MJS*

ASHCHURCH: The Tewkesbury platform, after the tracks had been lifted, is seen here on 30 September 1967. The boarded access to the station has been utilised by the Ford Popular on the platform, to the rear of which the sign still points 'round the corner' for 'Parcels and Goods Enquiries'. What looks to be a group of enthusiasts are enjoying the run of the place. One wonders what delights lay behind the attractive bay window at this end of the station building!

Hardly conceivable as the same location, the tall pine is the only common feature still visible from the 'past' view. On 3 August 2007 a footbridge still spans the tracks, not the aesthetically pleasing original, however, but a far uglier monstrosity that cost thousands more than might be deemed necessary, thanks to Health & Safety legislation! A telephone box stands by the new station entrance, while the rest of the scene is taken up with car park and Dowty Sport & Social Club built on the old site. With new industrial units out of site to the left, the access road to the station has been remodelled and widened. *John Edgington/MJS*

ASHCHURCH: Viewed from the southern end of the Tewkesbury platform, No 41900 pauses in the cattle dock, having run round its train before taking up position at the head of the next service over the branch on 7 March 1959. The road access, mentioned on the previous page, can be more clearly seen on the extreme right, with wooden fencing marking the boundary and shielding the small shed, which was probably the stable block in former times. Working from Bath Green Park at the birth of British Railways, subsequent allocations for No 41900 were to Lancaster, Longsight (Manchester) and Gloucester (Barnwood) – its home when pictured – from where the end came on 24 March 1962. The station master's house stands in the background.

The old stable building is still extant on 2 August 2006 – just – but in a dilapidated state, and, while visible on the ground, it is hidden in this view behind the van in the centre of the picture. The old access road is still visible, through the gateway to the right, but most is buried beneath the recent industrial development. The station master's house has been swept away, not least by the realignment of the A46 road and the provision of a new bridge slightly closer to the station site. Note the bus waiting shelter on the left; one distinct advantage of the station in the 21st century is the provision of a bus service to and from Cheltenham every 15 minutes. However, the journey, via Tewkesbury town centre, does take considerably longer than the train! *Gerald Adams, MJS collection/ MJS*

ASHCHURCH: Our last look at the Tewkesbury platform takes us to the northern end on 8 September 1949 to witness No 40116 waiting to leave with a train to Malvern. The gently escaping steam, driver talking to a bowler-hatted gentleman, doors open on the carriages and the family seemingly in no hurry to board, all give the impression of a relaxed atmosphere, without the constant rush and bustle so prevalent today. Another Barnwood locomotive at this time, the 2-6-2T moved to Bristol (Barrow Road) shed the following year, before departing in 1958 for Chester, Birkenhead and Bangor, being withdrawn from the latter on 1 December 1962.

The 'present' view shows the current car park area at Ashchurch on 3 August 2007. The identifying features are the A46 road bridge, albeit much enlarged and slightly closer to the camera than the original, and the old stable block shed, the roof of which peers over the hedgerow right of centre. This rapidly deteriorating structure can just be made out beyond the right-hand car, but the majority is hidden by the tree growth. Sadly, this present view is neither as peaceful nor as aesthetically pleasing as in the past! *H. C. Casserley, MJS collection/MJS*

ASHCHURCH: Part of the reason for Ashchurch being such a pivotal position in this part of north Gloucestershire can be seen in this view from 1949. At a time when the railways were still recovering from the devastation and privation wrought by the Second World War, but newly into Nationalisation, there remained many hundreds of miles of branch lines and main lines that served the nation at a time when road transport was still not a major competitor. To the right, a meandering service to Birmingham, via Redditch, waits to leave from the eastern branch platform, while on the more direct main line No 41097 has the road with a four-coach Birmingham-Gloucester local. Beyond the last coach of this train, an ex-MR 3F 0-6-0 waits in the loop with a freight. Note the clean lines everywhere, adding to the delights of the MR architecture, and the 'drunken' steps at the end of the bay platform!

Again that pine tree is an identifiable common denominator, together with the Birmingham-Bristol main line, but also still surviving are the ex-MR cottages – seen just to the right of the branch train in the 'past' view – now painted white. On 2 August 2006 it is good to portray a station still serving the local community, but as we have already seen this was not always the case. That huge footbridge dwarfs the more perfunctory waiting shelter, while beyond the nearside branch platform still remains, although swallowed by brambles and other greenery. A single track leads into the nearby MoD camp. *Joe Moss, Roger Carpenter collection/MJS*

ASHCHURCH: Turning through 180°, the lines into the Tewkesbury branch platform can again be seen to the right as 'Jubilee' No 45690 *Leander* roars non-stop through the station with a Bristol-Birmingham express in 1962. To the left is the relatively new 'Ashchurch Junction' signal box, opened on 27 July 1958. Life for this was brief, however, as it was closed on 16 February 1969, when control was passed to a new power box at Gloucester. Appearing from Crewe Works in March 1936 (Lot No 121 and Makers No 288), complete with name, *Leander* entered Nationalisation in 1948 working from Bristol (Barrow Road) shed, the principal shed in the area for ex-LMS locomotives. In common with a number of other class members, it stayed there throughout its BR career until withdrawal on 21 March 1964. It is here wearing the 82E shedplate appropriate to that depot from 1 February 1958. Happily, it escaped being scrapped, despite being stored at Dai Woodham's Barry Docks yard for just short of eight years! Salvation came with removal from the graveyard in May 1972, and it was restored to steam at the East Lancs Railway in 2002. Note the water column by the box for thirsty steam engines.

The racetrack that is the near-4-mile straight stretch through Ashchurch is well seen in this view from 2 August 2006. This shot has deliberately been taken without motive power to show more clearly the major changes here, including the new A46 road bridge that is now a few feet closer to the station than its predecessor. All evidence of this formerly being an important junction has gone, apart from just that one short stretch on the left that dives into the undergrowth to access the MoD camp. Elsewhere, everything has been wholly obliterated. *Joe Moss, Roger Carpenter collection/MJS*

ASHCHURCH: This truly delightful study of a branch-line train portrays an ex-GWR loco in the heart of LMS territory! No 8743 has run round its single-coach train and is caught by the afternoon sunshine as it is positioned ready to take the 4.30pm local to Evesham. The date is 15 May 1963, seven months after the cessation of passenger services beyond Evesham to Redditch, and only a month before this truncated traffic would also cease: Evesham to Ashchurch closed completely on 9 September of that year. A Gloucester engine when seen here, No 8743 went 'up to Lunnon' in January 1964 to be withdrawn from there ten months later.

The most obvious change over the ensuing 40 or so years is Mother Nature's reclamation act! Semaphores, lighting, station sign, footbridge and train have all gone, but the platform remains, as does the pine, now considerably bigger! The main line can just be seen beneath the new A46 bridge, with the erstwhile branch line still in place for that short run to the MoD camp. The new footbridge is prominent alongside the ragwort, teasels, brambles and wild sweet peas on 4 August 2007. *Ben Ashworth/MJS*

ASHCHURCH: Under the shelter of the station canopy, with the rain beating down – notice it bouncing from the train's box vans! – the photographer has captured the station in its twilight years. On 30 May 1969 D1689 heads south through distinctly unsummery weather conditions with an inter-regional fitted freight. Devoid of the branch lines for many years, the main-line station was to lose its own passenger services and be totally closed on 15 November 1971. The short metal and glass canopy of the down platform will only give limited respite from the inclement weather to waiting travellers! New from Brush on 21 November 1963 and initially allocated to Bristol (Bath Road) shed, D1689 became 47486 under TOPS in February 1974. Following a two-year spell at Wolverhampton (Oxley) shed from 1964 to 1966, it moved to the Midland Region from where it was withdrawn (serving Bescot depot by that time) on 6 July 1987.

The second view provides a real 'past and present' in one shot! Apart from the obviously new design of station, this view could have almost been from 30 years earlier! The weather is contriving to recreate the 'past' scene, but this time without the wet stuff as preserved D1015 *Western Champion* roars full throttle through Ashchurch at 0714 on 23 June 2007, handling 13 coaches unaccompanied at the head of Pathfinder Tours' 'The Cornishman' en route from Birmingham International to Penzance. New from Swindon Works in January 1963, the end came less than 14 years later, in December 1976, as BR decided to rid itself of diesel-hydraulics. Thankfully, salvation beckoned in the guise of the Diesel Traction Group and, as is evident from this view, it has been restored to main-line standards. Note that tree again, beyond the footbridge.
Robin Leleux/MJS

ASHCHURCH: Before finally leaving the station, which was indeed intricate in operation, we take a look at the layout immediately to the north. An ancient wooden-post signal, with a delightful finial, guards the flat crossing here, which gave direct access between the Tewkesbury and Evesham branches. Beyond that a siding ran into the turnout to the Dowty works area on the left, while on the down main line a three-way point gives access to and from the loops. In this view from 1949, looking north towards Worcester and Birmingham, the scene is 'open', with local housing visible.

The view nearly 60 years later shows some of the dramatic changes that have been wrought here. At 0814 on a sunny 6 August 2007, Virgin 'Voyager' No 221143 *August Picard* – new in October 2002 – approaches Ashchurch with 1V07, the VT 0655 Derby-Bristol Temple Meads service. The large water tower on the extreme left, the distant footbridge and the down loop are still present, but elsewhere everything has changed, not least with the industrial and housing development on the old Dowty site. The 1857 house in the middle of the 'past' picture still stands 150 years on, on Northway Lane, but is now lost from view from the station. *Joe Moss, Roger Carpenter collection/MJS*

ASHCHURCH: For a brief period Ashchurch had another claim to fame. Under the aegis of the Dowty Railway Preservation Society, there was an all-too-short-lived attempt at setting up a preservation centre. Containing many employees of the Dowty Group, the Society was set up in 1962. Various items of stock were assembled, including a 2-foot-gauge operational line within the company's site, but perhaps the most charismatic of items was No 46201 *Princess Elizabeth*. Built in 1933 at Crewe Works as No 6201, she was the second of the class that came to be affectionately known as 'Lizzies'. After withdrawal in 1962 she was bought by the then Princess Elizabeth Locomotive Society straight from BR. Initially kept at the Dowty Railway Preservation Society's premises at Ashchurch, she was subsequently moved to the Bulmers Railway Centre in Hereford. When that closed in the 1990s the loco moved to the East Lancs Railway. She is seen here in the mid to late 1960s in much the same livery as received from BR. On the right is Avonside 0-4-0T No 1977, in the Cadbury Bournville livery of its previous owner but awaiting a return to steam. Note the substantial Dowty building in the background, which, minus its upper part, still remains in 2007.

Access to the Dowty site was by a siding from the main line, inherited when the company took over the site. This can be seen on the left, and in the distance is the rear end of No 6201, close to the 'Iron Bridge' footbridge built by German POWs, perhaps awaiting her move to Bulmers. On the main line D1754 heads south with 1V79, the 'Devonian' express. In this undated view, thought to be the very early 1970s, the diesel was still young, having emerged from Brush Works in August 1964. Initially going to Landore depot, on the north-west outskirts of Swansea, it remained a BR(WR) loco until a move to the MR in September 1968. It was renumbered thereafter 'by decades', becoming No 47160 in February 1974, 47605 exactly ten years later, 47746 in March 1994 and sidelined in 2004! Happily, preservation beckoned and The Brush Type 4 Fund purchased it in February 2007. *Mervyn Mason, MJS collection/Paul Chancellor's collection*

73

TEWKESBURY was the only station in Gloucestershire on the Ashchurch-Great Malvern branch. The town was first joined to the emerging railway network from 21 July 1840, on a branch from Ashchurch as part of the Birmingham & Gloucester Railway empire; it was horse-worked until 18 February 1844! Situated between Oldbury Street and High Street, tracks crossed both roads, with an extension over the latter to Tewkesbury Quay.

When the branch was extended to Great Malvern, by way of a slight detour around and past the town, a temporary station was provided to the north-east of the original on 16 May 1864. This was, in turn, replaced by a much grander affair in 1872, whose frontage is seen here on 1 May 1956, as No 58071 shunts stock in the Malvern platform.

The branch line to Ashchurch was singled in 1958, then passenger services to both Ashchurch and Upton-on-Severn ceased on 14 August 1961 and the station was closed, although freight facilities survived until 2 November 1964. Some reports have it that the station was demolished shortly afterwards, but as can be seen from this view of 24 July 1968 the buildings were still extant and look to be in use. Nature is encroaching, a chimney pot has been removed, the posters have gone, as has most of the glass in the windows, but one gas lamp stands defiantly on the left.

Nearly forty years later nature has won the battle! On 12 August 2007, almost exactly 46 years after the last passenger train, amazingly the platforms still remain among the trees, although now disfigured to some extent by the growth of foliage. The trackbed remains as a footpath into Tewkesbury, and during the 2007 floods was virtually the only way into the town on foot! *H. C. Casserley/Robin Leleux/MJS*

TEWKESBURY: Away from the town centre and with the rest of the branch running through very rural scenery, passenger services were never over-stretched, apart from times of regattas, when rowers (and their boats) and others would come in by train. In latter years trains consisted of just a single coach, and that is all that is provided behind No 41900 in 1961, as the Upton-on-Severn to Ashchurch service pauses for possible custom shortly before closure. Note the large signal gantry, more gas lamps, the large girth of the telegraph pole and the equally grand gentlemen's convenience! A parcels trolley waits hopefully on the platform and the posters are in good shape, as is the sizeable canopy, almost reaching the train.

Another view from 24 July 1968 shows that the basic structures were intact, although nature was gaining a hold on both platforms and trackbed. Note the very low gasholder in the distance.

Finally, we are denied a view of the station! This is as close as the camera can come to portray anything material on 12 August 2007. We are very close to the erstwhile trackbed as it approached the station and the platforms begin just inside the right-hand 'black hole'! Though rounded by years of tree growth and occasional human access, they are still quite plainly in situ within the 'green tunnel', with the footpath between. *David Johnson/ Robin Leleux/MJS*

TEWKESBURY: Built on the north side of the Quay branch line, west of the original 1840 station, the engine shed for the town was a brick-built one-road affair, physically attached to the malthouse alongside Station Street – note the rooftops to the left. Opened with the line in 1840, it boasted a water column and coal stage and survived until closure by BR on 7 September 1962, latterly as a sub-shed to Gloucester (Barnwood). Thereafter it remained in industrial use until 1986, when it was demolished as part of 'The Maltings' residential development. On 3 September 1955 No 43754 stands partly inside the shed, while No 58071 pauses alongside; both were long-time regulars on the branch. Note the fire irons leaning against the wall and the roof of the malthouse being renewed.

By 10 July 1959 the area looks somewhat different, with the right-hand wall now much diminished in height and the track layout in front of the shed altered. On this date there are plenty of coal wagons, including those now empty on the coal stage (right), but no locomotives.

Whether deliberate or not, the construction of 'The Maltings' residential development has retained the basic outline of the old structure. This is seen overlooking yet another car park on railway land, which, on 12 August 2007, is also home to a plastic bottle bank, which is full to overflowing from the distribution of thousands of bottled water containers resulting from the recent flooding. The houses on the left, on Station Street, are a common link to all three views. It is indeed hard now to imagine the past usage of this area! *Norman Glover, F. A. Wycherley collection/ R. M. Casserley/MJS*

TEWKESBURY: A view further west has the engine shed just visible in the misty distance in February 1953. The houses in Station Street can just be made out to the left of No 45265, which is standing alongside the original 1840 platform. Immediately behind the loco the rails cross Oldbury Street and those in the foreground will go across High Street to the Quay. The 'Black Five' was larger than most of the motive power seen in and around the town and, individually, was almost unique in serving just one shed – Saltley in Birmingham – for the whole of its British Railways life. Withdrawal came on 19 May 1962. Note the general dilapidated air of this area of the railway at this date. *John Edgington*

MYTHE TUNNEL: North-west of Tewkesbury station, on the run to Upton-on-Severn and beyond, the line ran under the Worcester-bound A38 road at its junction with the A438 to Ledbury. This was accommodated by the boring of a 420-yard tunnel, and the northern portal is seen on 16 May 1957, as the ubiquitous No 43754 emerges with the 5.10pm Ashchurch to Upton-on-Severn service. Apparently running 'wrong line', the nearside track was disused at this time. This ex-MR 0-6-0 was another engine that stayed put, being officially shedded at Gloucester (Barnwood) throughout British Railways days and spending much of its time running up and down this branch. Its end came on 26 January 1963.

Yes, this *is* the same place! The trackbed can just be made out as the area not swamped by tree growth and the tunnel entrance is centre right, though bricked up nowadays. Obviously not an area regularly visited by enthusiasts, it is nevertheless a quiet spot in which to take a break and dream of past events! *Hugh Ballantyne/MJS*

Ex-GWR lines north from Gloucester

GLOUCESTER (HORTON ROAD): Returning to Gloucester and former GWR metals before we sprint north to Cheltenham, this picture is enclosed for no better reason than it both starts our second journey north and is 'a damned fine picture'! On a bright sunny summer's day, Nos 7307 and 5545 are nearest the camera. The latter is about to run onto the turntable on 3 July 1964, with the fireman waiting to accept the challenge of turning it! Elsewhere there is a mix of GWR, LMS and BR Standard types, and the whole, exuding as it does an air of prosperity and confidence, is the epitome of the appeal of steam and steam sheds. *Ben Ashworth*

CHELTENHAM (LANSDOWN JUNCTION): We have already visited Lansdown Road station in the last chapter, but this time we are tracing the traffic along the ex-GWR route through the town. Seen from the southern extremity of the former LMS facility, No 6137 prepares to bypass the station on 14 July 1962 as it heads north on the last stage of its journey as the 1.25pm Kingham-Cheltenham St James stopper. Closure of the latter station came in 1966. Lansdown Junction is beyond the bridge, and the route from Kingham can be seen through the left arch. No 6137 was a much-travelled loco, at various times serving Old Oak Common, Bristol (Bath Road), Tyseley and Stourbridge Junction sheds. At the time of this photo it was allocated (not surprisingly) to Gloucester (Horton Road).

The location is obviously the same, but the passage of time has not been kind to the railway here. The trackbed used by No 6137 was lifted some time after 1966, but is still obvious here, together with the retaining wall (now covered by greenery). The sidings of the LMS route on the right have both gone, signalling changes have seen semaphores disappear and rationalisation with the introduction of colour lights, and the growth of trees and bushes on either side of the railway has been prodigious. On 28 June 2006 No 66195 approaches Lansdown station on a northbound freight. *Edwin Wilmshurst/MJS*

CHELTENHAM MALVERN ROAD was late joining Cheltenham's railways. Though the site of what was to become the station was a railway location from 1847, when a broad gauge line was laid from Lansdown, and in greater active service from 1881, when the branch to Bourton-on-the-Water was opened, it was not until the 'Honeybourne Line' from the north joined to St James, thus creating a north-south through route, that Malvern Road was opened, on 30 March 1908. This early 1960s view from Malvern Road itself, looking south, shows the curving nature of the track through the station and the extensive sidings to the right, which also housed the engine shed (extreme right); however, the sidings are becoming overgrown and the bay platform has lost its rails. A train is due from the south.

The whole of the former trackbed from Lansdown to St James is now a footpath/cycleway and is seen here on 10 August 2006. Other than the rough approximation of the curvature of the old route, it is barely conceivable that this is the same place. The road bridge parapet is shown in the foreground, to give some relief to the mass of leaves! The old sidings are now occupied by various industrial buildings. *Lens of Sutton collection/MJS*

CHELTENHAM MALVERN ROAD is seen again, looking north towards St James, on 6 April 1953. The advert for Brylcreem predominates on the wall of the rather ugly building on the left, while beyond are the Gents, the Ladies Room and the General Waiting Room. At the far end a couple wait for their train, while on the right goods wagons await their next duty.

The delightfully ornate Malvern Road bridge, in the distance of the 'past' view, is still just visible on 10 August 2006, beyond the cyclist. The tree-lined route is pleasant enough for walkers/cyclists but without the charm of yesteryear, although the retaining wall on the right does give a flavour. There has also been an attempt to provide a semblance of the past with the edging stones on the left mimicking the former platform edge. *Lens of Sutton collection/MJS*

Below Moving to the Malvern Road end of the station, on a day around 1960, the bay platform is still rail connected and designated 'Platform 2'. The sidings, too, look clean and the whole, with the enamel running-in sign, gives the impression of being ready for the next job. *Lens of Sutton collection*

CHELTENHAM MALVERN ROAD: These two photographs provide close-up views of the bay platform. On 8 February 1953 a Birmingham Locomotive Club special, from Birmingham to Swindon, has paused at the station for members to alight, stretch their legs and view the facilities. Presumably railcar W14W is about to set off again, as most of the participants appear to be back on board, with one or two stragglers making their way along the platform and the railman patiently waiting for them to rejoin so that they can continue. Built by Gloucester RCW in 1936 and capable of seating 70 persons, W14W was withdrawn towards the end of the 1950s, spending much of its later years in and around Leamington Spa.

Six years later, on 23 May 1959, more conventional motive power is on display in the bay, having arrived with a two-coach evening local. Taken at precisely 6.03pm, from a train leaving for the north, the shadows are lengthening but the bright evening sunshine picks out the details of No 9445, its crew and onlookers. Just eight years old when photographed, though derived from a more ancient GWR design, No 9445 was another example serving just one shed – Gloucester (Horton Road). Withdrawn on 27 February 1960, it was a victim of changing needs but, at less than nine years old, was a tragic waste of public expenditure. *John Edgington/Michael Mensing*

CHELTENHAM ST JAMES: And so we arrive at the terminus at St James. Much closer to the heart of Cheltenham than the town's other stations, the fact of it being a terminus was its ultimate downfall following the opening of the 'Honeybourne Line' through route in 1908, which bypassed the station. Originally opened in 1847 as a broad gauge extension from Lansdown, it saw services to Bourton-on-the-Water from 1881, then, a decade later, through services to Southampton by way of the newly constructed M&SWJR south from Andoversford. This delightful view of the station, yard and approach lines from the through route, taken on 7 May 1964, seems to indicate a situation in rude health, with an unidentified train leaving for Kingham. Beyond the station are the spire of St Mary's Church and the substantial tower of St Matthew's.

The station closed in January 1966, and when your author first visited the site, in the early 1980s, it was a public but somewhat ad hoc car park, with neither markings nor surfacing. As can be seen from this 10 August 2006 view, much of it is still in use as a car park, but now properly laid out as part of the Waitrose supermarket development. Confirmation that this is the same view is provided by St Mary's spire, and the title of the apartments being built on part of the land on the left. *Ben Ashworth/MJS*

CHELTENHAM ST JAMES: As mentioned opposite, Cheltenham was linked to Southampton from 1891, thanks to the opening of the M&SWJR. This brought greater motive power variety into the town, initially with the new railway's own engines, but in latter days ex-SR locos reached this far north. One such example is seen here on 20 February 1960, as No 31629 makes a spirited exit from St James with the 1.52pm train to Southampton. Meanwhile a GWR tank prepares to run round its train from Kingham. As with most ex-SR locos working this route, No 31629 was shedded to Eastleigh, but it had previously operated from Guildford and Nine Elms. A move to Norwood Junction, south of London, came on 19 November 1962, from where it faced the cutter's torch from 27 January 1964.

The platform from which No 31629 is leaving is on the right of this 9 October 1965 view. On the left a more modern type waits to leave with an even longer through train: 'Hymek' diesel-hydraulic D7055 enjoys some evening autumn sunshine before leaving with the 5.20pm through train to Paddington. Note the two churches still dominant in the background, and that the station name board does not specify 'St James' to avoid any potential confusion! D7055 is just short of three years old at this stage, at the height of its powers, but further life would be short, with withdrawal coming in April 1973. It was, however, granted a slight reprieve, being transferred into Departmental Stock as TDB968004 before finally being dispensed with. *John Edgington/Edwin Wilmshurst*

Above CHELTENHAM ST JAMES: The substantial goods shed seen in 1964 on the extreme right of the upper view on page 84 is here seen in close-up ten years earlier. This official photograph, taken by the Civil Engineer's Office Photographic Department of BR(WR) on 3 August 1954 – your author's 11th birthday! – shows a variety of constructional styles, materials and dates. An advert for Levers Cattle Foods adorns the nearest shed. The dull weather does nothing to lighten the effect of years on the materials and the whole area looks a little down at heel. Freight services continued at St James until late 1966. Notice St Mary's spire again craning for attention! *MJS collection*

Below Great Western Road crossed the 'Honeybourne Line' immediately north of the junction for St James station and close to the throat of the station yard. An appropriate express engine is seen about to pass under the road, as an unidentified ex-GWR 'Castle' 4-6-0 approaches the adverse Distant signal at the head of the southbound 'Cornishman' express on 7 September 1962. With housing close to both sides of the railway, it is not hard to understand that some had to be demolished in 1906 to allow the line into the town by this route. The new Mini, the cloth-capped gentleman sauntering slowly down Great Western Road and the sunshine all combine to make a delightful portrait. *Ben Ashworth*

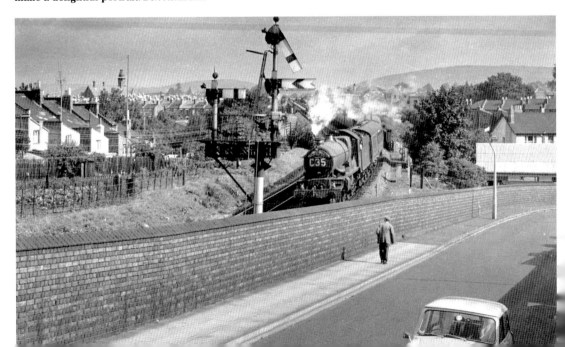

CHELTENHAM RACECOURSE: A couple of miles north of the town is Prestbury Park, Cheltenham's famed racecourse. Such was the growth in its popularity and the clamour for people to more easily travel to race days that a station was built next to the course and opened on 13 March 1912. Situated in a cutting, with the railway passing under the A435 road to Evesham immediately to the south, it was sensibly provided with two 700-foot platforms to accommodate the long trains needed, especially during the March 'Cheltenham Festival'. On 15 August 1964 No 5042 *Winchester Castle* leaves the station with the 3.55pm Leamington Spa General-Gloucester Central stopping service. Significant of the times, when front-line locomotives were increasingly relegated to more servile duties, the 'Castle' has been demoted to just three coaches and has obviously not received much external 'TLC' in the recent past! It was withdrawn less than a year later, on 11 June 1965.

One of the treasured aims of the Gloucestershire Warwickshire Railway when it took over the route south from Toddington was to re-open as far as Racecourse. Much effort and many years later, it achieved that goal, the occasion being celebrated by HRH Princess Anne on 7 April 2003. This view on 10 August 2006 shows the track immediately south of the station, with run-round facilities. The next goal in this direction is to strike closer to the town, and though the signals are installed here in anticipation of use in the near future, they will be an aid for the future, too. It is difficult to imagine that this was once been part of a north-south express route! *Michael Mensing/MJS*

CHELTENHAM RACECOURSE: While both platforms were graced with decorative pre-fabricated wooden buildings, largely housing waiting and toilet facilities, the entrance to the up Platform 1 had an additional roadside facility, containing booking office and hall, cloakroom and waiting room. Happily, this was not demolished on closure on 19 March 1976 and has been retained as a feature by the restorationists. This is the view on 24 July 1968, when it was advertising connections for 'Gloucester, Stroud, Swindon, Paddington, Hereford and South Wales'! Note the A435 to the left and the cattle grid on the access road to the racecourse on the right.

As seen on 10 August 2006, the situation is remarkably little changed! The metal fencing is extant, as is the building's canopy and the steel roofing, designed to give the impression of slate! Renovation and repainting has occurred, however, and a new entrance created at the end of the fencing on the right. The old access road has gone, with new fencing installed. A Ford Focus stands by the building, both overseen by the trees on either side of the railway, now considerably taller than before. *Robin Leleux/MJS*

CHELTENHAM RACECOURSE: Down on the platform we look back towards Cheltenham through the road bridge along part of the two 700-foot-long platforms. The main entrance from the road is seen to the left, with the slightly less defined but equally steep pathway to the up platform to the right. The fixture below the Platform 1 sign is interesting. Resembling a race starter's platform, its precise purpose is unknown – was it a platform for a ticket collector to operate at the foot of the incline? Although an undated view, the photographic evidence appears to indicate a period around the late 1950s/early 1960s.

The early decorative pre-fabricated buildings mentioned on page 88 have not been faithfully recreated by the new railway, but an attractive waiting shelter has been provided and the opportunity has been taken to incorporate part of it in the 'present' view, taken on 10 August 2006. The down platform has been temporarily lost beneath the trees, but the up one has been fully restored. The access slope to the far platform is still there, should future traffic conditions dictate the rebuilding of that side. Currently the second track merely acts as a run-round for this (hopefully temporary) terminus. At the far end of this nearside platform, just before the bridge, a large water tank has been rescued from Clifford station and installed for thirsty locos! *Great Western Trust collection/MJS*

CHELTENHAM RACECOURSE: As previously mentioned, this line was an express route between Birmingham and Gloucester, but it was also strategically important for freight traffic, much of it being south-west to north-east. On an unknown date in June 1965 No 92224 heads a rake of coal empties northwards through the station. New as late as 14 June 1958, the 9F was initially allocated to Banbury shed. Thereafter it remained a BR(WR) loco until a move was made to Speke Junction, near Liverpool, on 13 August 1966. Withdrawal from there was on 7 October 1967, late in steam days on BR. The painted 'shedplate' here is '2D', denoting a second spell at Banbury.

Unable to access the end of the platform, this is a comparative view from 10 August 2006, showing No 35005

Canadian Pacific running round its train before returning to Toddington as the 1305 departure from Racecourse. The coaching stock and passengers wait patiently in Platform 1. The prodigious tree growth is again obvious. *Gerald Adams, MJS collection/MJS*

BISHOPS CLEEVE: Once virtually surrounded by orchards, the transport of fruit – and cattle – became an important source of income for the station. In the early years of the 20th century passenger numbers were also healthy, but, as with so many other areas of the UK, declining traffic saw closure, this time on 7 March 1960 (for passengers) and 1 July 1963 (for freight). On 16 August 1958 No 6819 *Highnam Grange* steams northwards on a Cardiff-Birmingham express. The very attractive signal box, with wooden superstructure on Cleeve Hill Quarry stone, had 31 levers – but never used them all – and closed on 11 August 1965. The goods shed, in right distance, closed on 1 July 1963. The end for the 'Grange' came at Worcester on 15 January 1966. *Henry Priestley, Milepost 92½ collection*

91

BISHOPS CLEEVE: Our first view of the station proper is from a more distant era and a world since much changed. On 5 September 1932, looking north, the weather is dry but rain showers are expected, judging by the overcoat over the gentleman's arm (right) and the lady with her umbrella (left). Opened on 1 June 1906, with the completion of the Winchcombe-Bishops Cleeve section of the 'Honeybourne Line', it was for two months a terminus before the next section south was opened. When new it was on the eastern edge of the village it served, on the road to Woodmancote, but despite the neighbouring orchards being built on and housing surrounding the station, closure to passengers still came relatively early, on 7 March 1960.

Crossing to the down platform and looking back towards Cheltenham on 27 February 1960, No 9727 pulls into the station with a northbound local, just ten days before the end for passengers. Note the use of Cleeve Hill Quarry stone for the station buildings, and the photographer's briefcase on the grass-covered platform. No 9727 had been a Gloucester (Barnwood) engine for more than a decade when seen here but, after the closure of this route to local traffic, it was transferred to Cardiff (Canton) on 22 April 1961. Its demise was from Barry less than two years later, on 9 February 1963.

The restorationists of the Gloucestershire Warwickshire Railway have worked hard to restore the railway to Cheltenham, as we have already seen. Much unseen effort was needed and some of this can be judged in this view from 20 July 1997, when the track had reached a point just north of Bishops Cleeve. *Clarence Gilbert, Roger Carpenter collection/ Edwin Wilmshurst/MJS*

GOTHERINGTON: Looking north towards Winchcombe on 5 September 1932, the station is trim and tidy, with yet more attractive Cleeve Hill Quarry stone for the main buildings on the left and the smaller waiting shelter on the right. Set about a mile from the eponymous village, in the middle of nowhere and away from the nearby country road, it is perhaps surprising that the station was provided with a siding capable of holding 22 wagons, a 6-ton crane and a 15-ton weighbridge. The view here, complete with platform gardens and advertising, certainly has the air of a station ready for business.

Another view from 10 August 2006 shows how wonderfully the present owner of the station buildings has recreated a stunning picture of an ex-GWR wayside station and a superb pictorial complement for the Gloucestershire Warwickshire Railway. The whole of the scene on both sides of the track has been restored and/or recreated by him, with the exception of the waiting shelter on the right, and he has helped to produce a wonderful haven of railway peace and tranquillity. *Clarence Gilbert, Roger Carpenter collection/MJS, with permission*

GOTHERINGTON: A little over a mile north of Bishops Cleeve, Gotherington station was also opened on 1 June 1906 but, serving a much more sparse and rural community, passenger numbers were never great, actually reaching their peak in 1913! Not surprisingly, therefore, closure came even earlier than its southern neighbour, on 13 June 1955; it had been unstaffed, and therefore classed as a halt, from 1 January 1941. This view, looking south towards Cheltenham, dates from 5 September 1932 and shows the main station buildings and signal box on the right-hand platform.

Seventy-four years later, and celebrating a centenary of railway here, the scene is both the same and different! After closure both platforms were demolished and one also lost its buildings. Happily for us today, the main buildings on the other platform survived, are now in private hands and have since been restored to glory. This 10 August 2006 view shows the platforms, but much shorter, and no trains call on this side. The station buildings have seen much 'TLC'. The operational side, again with a waiting shelter, now has a platform with edging stones that originally came from Withington station on the M&SWJR. *Clarence Gilbert, Roger Carpenter collection/MJS, with permission*

GREET TUNNEL: On the southern approach to Winchcombe, the railway runs through the 697-yard Greet Tunnel, the only such structure on the line and also the summit of the route between Stratford-upon-Avon and Cheltenham. On 26 June 1965, hauling one of just a handful of steam-operated summer Saturday holiday trains at the time, No 70045 – formerly *Lord Rowallan*, but here without its nameplates – bursts from the tunnel with the 11.10 Ilfracombe-Wolverhampton Low Level express. New on 19 June 1954, as one of the premier BR Standard express locomotives, it led a nomadic life, before an untimely end close to the end of steam on BR, on 30 December 1967.

Doing its best to mimic the 'Britannia', No 35005 *Canadian Pacific* is, sadly, not working quite as hard on 10 August 2006 and thus has not burst from the tunnel mouth, while the crew have time to momentarily relax and enjoy the view from the cab. Visiting the preserved railway for a spell, the 'Merchant Navy' certainly did much to recreate some of the scenes of the former main line, albeit now only a single track, and no doubt the passengers on this 1120 train returning to Toddington from Cheltenham Racecourse enjoyed the experience. Note how vegetation has grown, disguising the shoulder of the embankment. *Michael Mensing/MJS, with permission*

WINCHCOMBE: Swinging round to follow *Lord Rowallan* and its holiday summer Saturday journey north on 26 June 1965, we glimpse Winchcombe station through the road overbridge. With the escape of steam between chimney and smoke deflector, the driver is obviously obeying the 'SW' (sound whistle) notice! Initially based at Holyhead, for through expresses to Euston such as the 'Irish Mail', No 70045 stayed at that outpost for 5½ years before having seven different homes in the ensuing three years, including a nine-month spell on the GCR! When seen here it was a week into a seven-month stay at Oxley (Wolverhampton) shed, from where it travelled north to Carlisle (Kingmoor), its final home.

Again, verdant growth has softened the landscape, but the distant hills and the road bridge – newly rebuilt – are common to both views. No 35005 again recreates the 'past' view on 10 August 2006, even down to the maroon coaching stock! *Michael Mensing/MJS, with permission*

WINCHCOMBE: A mile north of the town it served – on the B4078 at Greet – Winchcombe was, nevertheless, the most important station between Cheltenham and Toddington. Opened on 1 February 1905, with the completion of the section from the last-named station, it boasted a full range of passenger and freight facilities, complete with 6-ton crane, and had three long sidings in a large goods yard to the east of the station. One of these served a cattle dock, with much trade coming from the nearby cattle market. On Cheltenham race days the sidings were also used to store coaching stock. Looking north, this is the view on 27 February 1960, showing the canopies on both platforms and the equally protected footbridge.

Sadly, on the renovated station the same protection is not given to those wishing to cross between platforms! However, at least both platforms have been reinstated, following the swift removal of the originals following the closure of the goods yard in November 1964, with the down one on the left now longer than previously. As seen on 10 August 2006, the station nameboard has been 'restored', as has a signal box at the far end of the platform, but for safety reasons the former barrow crossing has not been replicated. The new railway has made great strides over the past two decades in recreating this important station, in addition to the progress onwards to Cheltenham. *Edwin Wilmshurst/MJS, with permission*

WINCHCOMBE: Something of just how much had been achieved but how much was still to be done by the restorationists can be seen in this view from 31 March 1991. No 7752 arrives at the station with the 1500 Toddington-Gretton train; the latter station, some mile-and-a-half south of Winchcombe, was the southern terminus at the time. The down platform has been rebuilt and tracks laid in the goods yard once more, together with the erection of a new signal box, ready for the future. Semaphore signals are in situ but not yet in use. To the left, the Toddington platform is under construction. Rudimentary seating has been provided and a telephone box has appeared, Tardis-like, on the platform! Built in 1930 at the North British Locomotive Company's Glasgow works, No 7752 was withdrawn by BR on Boxing Day 1959 but survived destruction by sale to London Transport. Renumbered LT94, it was preserved after disposal by LT in 1971 and spends much time based at Tyseley, making occasional forays to other railways. *Tom Heavyside*

Above WINCHCOMBE: Back in time, we are now looking south on 7 September 1959 and see No 6868 *Penrhos Grange* on an unidentified northbound express, with chalked code '560' on the smokebox front. Still in apparently fine shape, the station was to close, with the rest of the local stations, just six months later. No 6868 was shedded at Taunton when pictured, but 5 November 1960 would see moves further south-west, including Cornwall. Further reallocations came on 6 October 1962 (to Didcot) and 2 November 1963 (to Oxford) before redundancy removed it from stock on 7 October 1965, hit by the increasing dispensation of steam by BR(WR). *Henry Priestley, Milepost 92½ collection*

Below Turning through 180° to look towards Toddington, another special train is captured passing the station. On 10 September 1961 No 7808 *Cookham Manor* has left Birmingham Snow Hill at 9.40am with 'X06', the SLS (Midlands Area) 'Farewell to the M&SWJ Railtour', and makes its way along the 'Honeybourne Line' en route to Cheltenham Malvern Road, the M&SWJR through Swindon Town and finally Andover Junction, before a return later in the day. Another widely travelled engine, No 7808 was under Tyseley's wing here, but three more moves were to come before withdrawal from Gloucester (Horton Road) on 15 January 1966 (a fortnight after the official end of steam on the ex-GWR system) and preservation thereafter. *Alan Donaldson*

NORTH OF WINCHCOMBE: These two views show the railway approaching the A46 road, just north of Winchcombe station, on 12 June 1965. In the first, positioning himself for the special he had come to photograph (see below), the photographer has not ignored a preceding train. Looking very much the worse for wear – a fact not helped by the very dull weather conditions! – No 92111, sans front numberplate, heads south with a rake of what looks to be loaded iron ore wagons. In view of its general condition, the 9F could be expected to be prone to rough riding, but there seem to be no problems, with the smoke clean, little waste steam and the fireman leaning casually from the cab. New in December 1956, to Cricklewood shed, No 92111 gradually moved up the Midland main line, through Leicester and Kirkby-in-Ashfield, before moving to the Liverpool area in 1964. It was

working from Birkenhead when captured here.

With the freight out of the way, the line was clear for No 44777 at the head of 1X82, the Warwickshire Railway Society's 'Somerset & Dorset Joint and Eastleigh Tour'. Starting from Birmingham Snow Hill, the special ran to Bath Green Park, Bournemouth Central and Eastleigh Works, before returning to Birmingham via Oxford. Locomotives used during the day, in addition to the 'Black Five', were Nos 92238, 34097 *Holsworthy* and 6967 *Willesley Hall*. Only minutes after this shot, No 44777 was clocked at 78mph through Cheltenham Racecourse station!
Both John Spencer Gilks

HAYLES ABBEY HALT was opened late in comparison to other stations on the route, on 24 September 1928. There must have been little real anticipation of much traffic, as it was situated midway between the villages of Didbrook and Hailes, again in glorious isolation in open countryside and close to the remains of the 13th-century Cistercian abbey after which it was named; the railway always insisted on its own way of spelling the name! The platforms were but 150 feet long, with corrugated iron waiting shelters, a path on either side from the road bridge and oil lamps hung from hooks bolted to a post! On 27 February 1960, ten days from the end of this service, No 1424, liberally spraying water from the tank, restarts the 1.17pm train from Honeybourne to Cheltenham, with auto-trailer W238W in tow.

The station closed in 1960, along with others on the route, and the platforms, footpaths and all trace of a station were swept away thereafter. There has been talk of resurrecting a halt here on the preserved Gloucestershire Warwickshire Railway, but nothing has happened as yet. This is the present-day view, captured on 31 March 1991; No 7752 is again seen, hauling the 1300 Toddington-Gretton service. At least there is still space to relay a second track, should the railway ever decide, like the Great Central Railway, that it was desirable and practical. *Hugh Ballantyne/Tom Heavyside*

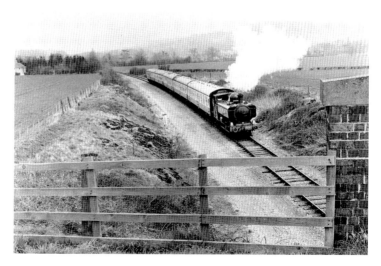

TODDINGTON: 27 February 1960 must have been a popular day for enthusiasts to visit the area, with passenger services due to disappear ten days later! No 9727, already caught by a different photographer at Bishops Cleeve on the same day, has now arrived at Toddington with the 1.00pm Cheltenham-Broadway local stopper. As was so often the norm in BR days, with the pride of the staff there until the last, stations about to close were kept spick and span, with, as seen here on the left, gardens trended to the last minute! The station opened on 1 December 1904 to the east of Toddington village, and was accessed from the B4077 road to Stow on the Wold. The Gloucestershire Warwickshire Railway re-opened it on 22 April 1984. It was and is a fine example of early 20th century GWR country station design, with thought and concern for the railway's customers and an eye for architectural aesthetics. *Hugh Ballantyne*

TODDINGTON: Looking north towards Broadway in the late 1970s, the end looks in store for the site. Services have ended, track will be lifted within a couple of years and all is abandoned. The single-storey main station building on the left carried a metal-framed glazed canopy that gave ample protection for waiting travellers; it housed the station master's office, booking office, general waiting room, a ladies' waiting room and toilets. The large wooden screen protecting the Gents from embarrassed eyes can be seen on the left painted white. A metal panelled footbridge was erected in 1912 but had been removed some years before this view. Note the massive water tank, provided to supply both station and locos.

Plus ça change … but thankfully much remains the same! A wonderful recreation of the station at its peak and a real credit to all involved, it is seen minutes before a downpour on 10 August 2006! The large water tank has disappeared, as has the running in board on the far platform, but elsewhere so much more has been added to enhance the original. Tasteful painting, hanging baskets, a functioning station clock, fire buckets, milk churn and well-kept platform surfaces all add to the ambience and 'feel-good factor' for the visiting public. *Great Western Trust collection/MJS*

TODDINGTON: While most 'past and present' comparisons feature the pre-preservation, working railway, there are times when 'work in progress' on preserved lines is equally interesting. Hence this view, on 6 September 1987, when the railway used whatever motive power was to hand and the run was so much shorter than subsequently. Built in 1936, Peckett saddle-tank No 1976 pulls into the platform, rather grandly bearing a 'Winchcombe Pioneer' headboard, celebrating the fact that services to that temporary terminus are only a month old! On this platform, the station building is in the early days of restoration, without the level of facilities now available. Beyond is another industrial steam loco, together with an ex-BR 'Teddy Bear' diesel.

Nineteen years later, on 10 August 2006, progress is obvious. On the far platform lawns have replaced the rougher ground and period lights and seats have been provided. On this side, seats and lights are accompanied by hanging baskets and 'ancient' artefacts in the guise of large period suitcases. There is also now a shop to encourage visitors to part with their money! Note the slightly unusual water tank at the platform end, which the author believes had previously been at Ashford, Kent. *Tom Heavyside/MJS*

TODDINGTON: The date is September 1970 and, ten years after the end of local passenger services, both platforms and footbridge have been removed, but the buildings, including the goods shed, all now abandoned, stand defiant. With threatening skies looming over the north Gloucestershire hills in the distance, an unidentified 'Peak' Class 45 heads north with inter-regional train 1M91. The first 60 of the class built in 1960/61 – 20 at Derby and 40 at Crewe concurrently – had the split route indicator boxes, positioned on either side of a central gangway. The next 66 – 18 from Derby and the rest from Crewe in 1961/2 – were refined in that the central gangway was dispensed with, leaving a plain front end between the boxes. The example here is from this later batch and is, therefore, numbered somewhere between D32-67 and D108-137.

An appreciation of just how much has been achieved since the early 1980s, in restoring not just a railway but also a real quality product to Toddington, can be judged from this view from 10 August 2006. Platforms and footbridge are restored, the buildings have been made fit for 21st-century use, and the station is again able to accommodate long passenger trains and their passengers. Out of sight at the head of the train, No 35005 *Canadian Pacific* seems impatient to be off, one minute from the 1030 departure time! *John Spencer Gilks/MJS*

STANWAY VIADUCT: Seen previously on page 95 approaching Winchcombe on 26 June 1965, No 70045 *Lord Rowallan* is caught in action again, travelling south six weeks later on 7 August 1965, having just crossed Stanway Viaduct, north of Toddington and very close to the Gloucestershire border. Still without nameplate and in despicable condition, it has plenty of steam available as it heads the Saturdays-only Wolverhampton-Ilfracombe holiday express. Crossing a valley in the undulating terrain, the highest of the viaduct's 15 arches is 42 feet and the whole span is 210 yards. Begun in 1903, it suffered the collapse of four arches seven months into construction, with four fatalities. Extra supports were then provided.

   The same vantage point is now hindered by undergrowth, so this view is slightly closer to the viaduct. On 10 August 2006 the railway had been celebrating the recent completion of track laying across the structure and thoughts were turning to further progress northwards to Broadway. Part of the works train is still on site and more ballasting is needed before trains can run over here. *Bryan Hicks/MJS, with permission*

Cheltenham to Stow-on-the-Wold and Moreton-in-Marsh

CHELTENHAM SOUTH & LECK-HAMPTON: Concurrent with the opening of the Bourton-on-the-Water to Cheltenham section of the Banbury & Cheltenham Railway, this station was opened on 1 June 1881. Sited to the south of the town centre and just north of the village of Leckhampton, it received a boost when the M&SWJR opened in 1891. Built in a cutting by the B4070 road into the town, initially just as 'Leckhampton', it became 'Cheltenham South & Leckhampton' from 1 May 1906, in an attempt to woo travellers for Cheltenham to alight here from the Newcastle-Swansea cross-country services that used the line from Banbury and heading south-west bypassing the town's other stations. Platforms were lengthened at the same time to accommodate the longer trains. In the first view, from the late 1930s, looking east, the goods yard is in the distance beyond the signal box at the platform end.

The name was changed again, to 'Cheltenham Leckhampton', in April 1952 and remained thus until closure ten years later on 15 October 1962. This view from the early 1960s shows the name change, and the goods yard by now occupied by Bloodworths industrial building. The main station building was behind the photographer, on this platform.

The only things that link the 'present' view with the 'past' are the general trajectory of the trackbed mirrored by the road and the trees on the right, still flourishing though restrained now with a retaining wall. As seen on 28 June 2006, the area has suffered the fate of so many former railway sites, turned over to industrial and car parking use. *Lens of Sutton collection (2)/MJS*

CHELTENHAM SOUTH & LECKHAMPTON: Crossing to the other platform and looking westwards, No 4161 enters the station with the 10.50am Cheltenham St James-Kingham train on 13 October 1962, slowing for the stop, no doubt to the delight of the couple waiting on the platform, with services about to end! Though built to an established GWR design, No 4161 did not appear until the early days of Nationalisation, on 30 November 1948, initially working from Barry shed in South Wales. In very smart external condition, it is here allocated to Gloucester (Horton Road), where it had arrived on 8 September 1962, but it was a well-travelled engine. It had previously served Merthyr Tydfil, Tyseley, Wolverhampton (Stafford Road) and Stourbridge Junction, and went on to Hereford (May 1963) and Worcester (November 1964) till withdrawal on 15 January 1966.

It would certainly be difficult for a train to pass this way today! Another view from 28 June 2006 shows that the road bridge is still in existence but with the old trackbed beneath raised, so that the height of the bridge arch has been halved and access blocked. The station site is now subsumed beneath a modern flats development on the edge of the industrial site. *Michael Mensing/MJS*

ANDOVERSFORD TUNNEL: On its way to Andoversford, the railway ran under and then around the northern edge of Sandywell Park; 384 yards long, the tunnel was alongside the A40 road but hidden from it by the cutting. Seen first in 1923, looking east, Andoversford station is some half a mile further on and the park is above and to the right, with one small cottage just visible among the trees.

Four decades later the tunnel is seen in the last days of trains over the route. On 13 October 1962 No 4109 is not unduly taxed as it leaves the tunnel with the 11.18am Kingham-Cheltenham St James local service. Having spent a good part of its life in the South West, the 2-6-2T moved to Kidderminster in November 1958, Worcester in March 1959, and finally Gloucester (Horton Road) – its home when seen here – in October 1961. Despite its duties being reduced after closure of local routes in the early 1960s, it survived until 4 May 1964. Note the well-kept railway, right up to the end, and the growth of trees on all sides, hiding any view of the park.

Another four decades have seen yet more growth and encroachment of greenery on the cutting and trackbed. The tunnel still survives, now a storage area but without normal access. The brickwork can just be seen beyond the fencing on 20 July 2006. *Keith Jones collection, MJS collection/Michael Mensing/ MJS, with permission*

ANDOVERSFORD, 7 miles east of Cheltenham, was an important station at its height, acting as a junction for two routes – east to Kingham and south to Andover and Southampton. Both routes shared tracks from Cheltenham, and on 5 July 1958 No 5514 has just traversed that stretch with the 2.45pm Cheltenham St James-Kingham stopper. The 1902 goods loop is seen on the left, while the 1935 replacement of the original 1881 signal box peers over the leading coach. The up platform, into which No 5514 is arriving, was of blue bricks, while the down platform was of stone blocks! Typical of the type to handle the Kingham turns, No 5514 did not survive to the end of the line, being withdrawn on 5 November 1960.

Not immediately obvious as the same place, the two tall trees on the right give the game away. Seen in the bright summer sunshine of 20 July 2006, the 'executive' development that has been created on the site – appropriately called Pine Halt – certainly presents a very attractive alternative to the railway. The house for sale would be an ideal home for a rail enthusiast! *John Spencer Gilks/MJS*

ANDOVERSFORD: In an undated view, but close to the end, an unidentified '51XX' 2-6-2T pauses in the down platform with a Kingham-Cheltenham train. The main station buildings are on this platform, featuring the goods shed closest to the camera and the waiting room, etc, with a flat awning, slate roof and three tall chimneys, the latter in brick with cement rendering. Engine crew and station staff pose for their portrait.

Once again the trees on the left provide the constant, marking the boundary to the site as they have done for more than 50 years. On 20 July 2006 the current arrangement clearly shows the alignment of the railway, platforms and trackbed echoed by the green swards and the roadway. At the far end of the station the line used to cross the A40, but no more, as, just beyond the distant house, the bridge has been removed and the A40, now a trunk road, has been realigned. *MJS collection/MJS*

ANDOVERSFORD JUNCTION: The race is on! This view immediately to the east of Andoversford station shows the divergence of the two routes, controlled by Andoversford Junction signal box on the left. The date is July 1949, when both routes were still fully functional. To the left, No 3214 approaches the station stop with a Kingham-Cheltenham train, while to the right an unidentified Class '63XX' waits for its turn to head for Cheltenham with a freight from the M&SWJR line.

Incredibly, this is what has become of those two routes! Following closure of the lines the railway was ripped up and the A40 realigned to take the course of the M&SWJR line around the village of Andoversford, before regaining its original course some miles further on. A very fast road, a rare brief interlude between vehicles has been taken advantage of on 20 July 2006, to prevent any injury to your photographer! *Millbrook House collection/MJS*

NOTGROVE: A delightful picture of an ex-GWR wayside station at work! Resplendent in green livery with the second British Railways logo on its tanks, No 4100 pauses at Notgrove station with the 8.50am Cheltenham St James-Kingham stopping service on 15 September 1962, a month from the last day. Complete with a period-liveried chocolate and cream coach behind, No 4100 is about to pull forward for the driver to receive the single-line token from the railwayman on the platform. Opened on 1 June 1881, with the line, originally as 'Notgrove & Westfield', the name was shortened to just 'Notgrove' in June 1896. At 760 feet above sea level, it had the distinction of being the highest through station on the GWR system! Despite this, its buildings was constructed of wooden clapboard, with limited protection to waiting passengers from the overhang of the slate roof. Both building and travellers, therefore, cannot have enjoyed inclement weather! Note the substantial station master's house, upper right.

Today the site is home to the Notgrove Caravan Club. Seen on 4 September 2006, the site is well laid out, clean and tidy and obviously well cared for. The alignment of the trackbed is mirrored in the roadway, and the old station master's house is still in place, but has seen some adjustments to its outline over the years. One wonders how many of the campers appreciate the significance of where they are staying. *John Spencer Gilks/MJS, with permission*

NOTGROVE: Looking for all the world like a double-track railway, it is, sadly, just a long loop on a single-track branch. This view, from 3 March 1962, provides a fine portrait of the station complex, virtually unchanged since opening. The squat station building stands between a small wooden extension – complete with fire buckets – and a corrugated-iron shed. Just out of picture to the left was a small goods yard that included a shed, cattle pens and an 8-ton crane. Over a mile from the eponymous village – and much closer to the tiny hamlet of Westfield – access to the station was by a short lane from the B4068 road to Bourton-on-the-Water, the bridge for which can be seen in the distance.

The former station master's house stands proud in both views, but here, on 4 September 2006, the additions to the near side are more readily apparent. Elsewhere, all sign of a railway ever having been here has been successfully swept away by the caravan park – and note how it is now impossible to see the road bridge, due to tree growth, despite it being so high above the trackbed. *Edwin Wilmshurst/MJS*

A view now from the very last days! Almost as if in aspic, the site has been virtually untouched since closure, with signals still guarding the line and only the waiting shelter from the down platform having disappeared. On 8 May 1964, 18 months after the last train, an engineer's train has possession of the up road, initially to lift the goods yard, before work starts on the main station structures and tracks. The very rural aspect in which the station was positioned is obvious from this angle. *Ben Ashworth*

BOURTON-ON-THE-WATER was some 5 miles east of Notgrove. Flanked by Nissen huts and open fields, this view of the goods yard at Bourton, from the road from the town to the A429 Roman Road, is a wonderful portrait of such a facility as perpetuated by the GWR and an equally superb template for railway modellers. Seen in the early 1950s, the station is in the left background, with the tracks on the far side, and on the right is the approach road and weighbridge. A goods shed stands at the far end of the yard and one of the sidings, by the station building, has a ramp for end loading. An attractive structure, in Cotswold style to match local architecture, the station was, however, relatively new, dating from 1936, when it replaced a far more ornate and handsome affair from 1863, built on the opening of the line from Stow-on-the-Wold. The large water tank and signal box can also be seen.

With the road view no longer available and development within the yard itself, this view from 4 September 2006 is on the ground and slightly closer to the weighbridge. The latter, much reduced in size from its predecessor, is in the centre with the station building to the left, beyond the stone wall and metal gates. The site is now occupied and operated by Gloucestershire Highways Department. *Joe Moss, Roger Carpenter collection/MJS, with permission*

BOURTON-ON-THE-WATER: This undated view is probably from 1962, close to the end of passenger services on the line. The vantage point of the previous page can be seen as the hedge in the centre distance, between the goods wagon and the station building. No 6137 prepares to leave the up platform with a Cheltenham-Kingham service, a small knot of people saying goodbye to someone and the bespectacled porter in reverie prior to exchanging single-line tokens with the loco's fireman. Note the rudimentary power source for the lamp standard on the down platform! No 6137 was another well-travelled engine, its last 15 years seeing it gradually move from London to West Midlands sheds. At this time it was allocated to Gloucester (Horton Road).

An amazing survivor! While everything around it has been transformed by progressive development, the 1936 station building has survived, now acting as a semi-moribund store for the local Council. Looking very down at heel, rumours have abounded that it is to be demolished, but also that it is destined for use on an extension to the Gloucestershire Warwickshire Railway. It is to be hoped that it is preserved in some way, even though this side is not particularly architecturally outstanding. Note the house built across the trackbed in the distance, and the fact that the B-road into the village, formerly on a bridge over the tracks, has been lowered to rail height. *MJS collection/MJS*

BOURTON-ON-THE-WATER: Leaving the up platform on 29 September 1962, a fortnight from the end, No 5184 restarts the 10.50am Cheltenham St James-Kingham service, crossing with No 4101 on the 11.18am westbound working. The large water tower on the right had a swing arm for delivery of the water to waiting locos. When opened on 1 March 1862, the station was a terminus for the route from Kingham and it stayed that way until 1881, when the extension to Andoversford was completed. Between those two dates it enjoyed the facility of a one-road engine shed. The town being one of the largest on the route, and also a popular tourist destination, the station saw healthy traffic figures and the cattle dock in the goods yard was equally well used. The original station building was wooden, with highly elaborate barge-boards and extensive gardens. No 5184 was a Leamington Spa loco for many years, apart from two very short 'holidays' in the West Country, before moving to Gloucester (Horton Road) shed on 8 September 1962. It is therefore relatively new to this route, and lasted until 22 November 1964.

As can be seen from the view on 4 September 2006, the trackbed has been commandeered as road access for industrial units on the left and residential development on the right. The house now built over the trackbed is seen more clearly, left of centre. The lamp standard by the station canopy can be seen on the centre left-hand pavement. *Hugh Ballantyne/MJS*

BOURTON-ON-THE-WATER: Our final look at the station is from the road overbridge, looking north-west towards Stow-on-the-Wold. Trees planted by the railway in the 19th century are doing well and parts of the gardens underneath are still visible, although those on the platforms have been removed. On an undated spring day in the early 1950s, the station is enjoying a period of quiet in the weak sunshine. The goods shed, at the far end of the station, is seen more clearly here and, beyond, a signal gantry is just visible, at the point where the long loop into the station takes over from the single track.

As previously mentioned, the road bridge over the railway has been dispensed with and the way into the town now runs on the level. This is the junction with the former trackbed, now known as 'Meadow Way leading to Station Meadow and Kings Meadow'. The station canopy still stands defiant opposite the housing, and the entrance to the Council site has strict instructions! Two young ladies walk past the building, probably totally oblivious of its importance. *Joe Moss, Roger Carpenter collection/MJS*

STOW ON THE WOLD: While Ordnance Survey maps have the town name with hyphens, the railway was again perverse, preferring to refer to it without! This can be seen here on the station nameboard, rather shyly hiding behind seat and trees! Two miles north-west of Bourton, it was unlike its neighbour in being some way out of the town and down a long steep hill, there being a drop of some 300 feet between the two! Thus, despite the area being yet another 'honey-pot' for tourism, there was only a single track through the station and just one platform face. Like its neighbour, however, it just managed to celebrate 100 years of operations, opening on 1 March 1862 and closing to passengers on 15 October 1962. The original station building was half-timbered, with two-tone roof tiles and tall chimneys. The building seen here, however, dates from 1936, like that at Bourton, and the two stations were identical. Looking towards Bourton, in a scene from around 1957, No 4573 pauses at the station with yet another Cheltenham-Kingham service, watched by station master and porter.

Fifty years later the building survives, as part of a greater whole. The outline of the original stone structure can be made out in the darker shape on the right-hand portion of the current house. As can be seen from this view from 4 September 2006, the 1936 building has been heightened and the rest of the extension designed to tastefully tone in with the original and the local architecture. The extension has also swallowed the former platform, and No 4573 was standing roughly where the ivy on the house wall now flourishes. As with other locations already covered in this volume, many tons of earth have been employed to raise the level of the new garden from the trackbed and to successfully landscape away any vestige of the railway. *MJS collection/MJS, with permission*

STOW ON THE WOLD: Moving to the other end of the platform and now looking towards Kingham, some 4½ miles distant, the similarity to Bourton's station is more readily apparent. Captured during a quiet period in the late 1950s, the platform scene is here dominated by the larger canopy of the goods shed, which was added to the station in 1936. Next to it, closer to the camera, the slightly more diminutive signal box from the same period controls both the station and the two parallel sidings to the west, just out of the picture to the left – note the pointwork in the foreground. There appears to be a collection of suitcases on the platform; perhaps it is holiday time, and in those days before widespread car use it was not unusual for families to send their trunks on to their holiday destinations in advance of their own journeys. Note the bridge carrying the railway under the A424 road to Burford, which can just be seen to the right of the large tree beyond the platform end.

As can be seen in the left foreground, in another picture from 4 September 2006, the slope to the platform and part of the structure still remain in place. The large tree by the A424 also still survives, but the view of the road is now totally hidden. The extent of rebuilding and landscaping is also obvious. Again out of sight to the left of this picture, evidence of the two sidings is still apparent within a lawn area. The whole recreation has been very sympathetically handled, both with regard to the original building and subsequent aesthetics. *MJS collection/MJS, with permission*

ADLESTROP is probably best known for Edward Thomas's famous 1898 short poem about the unscheduled stop at the station by a train on which he was travelling; certainly, the station had a remarkably invisible existence otherwise! Opened on 4 June 1853, with the opening of the line from Oxford to Evesham, it served two localities – Oddington and Adlestrop – of which Adlestrop House was the major feature. Initially 'Addlestrop & Stow Road', it became just 'Addlestrop' on 1 March 1862, then, from 1 July 1883, the second 'd' was dropped. It was a remarkable survivor, remaining open until 3 January 1966. This view, looking south from the A436 road bridge towards Kingham on 16 August 1958, shows No 3805 approaching the station, which was on the other side of the bridge behind the photographer. The mixed consist behind the 2-8-0 is typical of the type of traffic that earned so much for our railways in their first 150 years.

The ensuing 50 years have not been kind to the station, but, incredibly, despite attempts at closure, the route has survived and into the 21st century has become a healthy lifeline between Oxford and Worcester. Indeed, the view from 4 September 2006 shows recent investment, with fresh track, metal sleepers and ballast evident on the up (left-hand) line. Sadly, much loved railway furniture such as semaphore signals and telegraph poles have gone, but at least the route still has double track and regular passenger services to and from Oxford and London. *MJS collection/ MJS*

ADLESTROP: Crossing the road bridge and now looking north towards Worcester, the wooden construction of the station building, necessitated by the financial constraints of the Oxford, Worcester & Wolverhampton Railway in the 1850s, is seen on 18 November 1961. Originally designed by Brunel, the work was completed by John Fowler. The large goods shed is here being passed by No 7018 *Drysllwyn Castle* as it steams southwards with a Hereford-Paddington express. One of the BR 'Castles', new on 31 May 1949, it spent the first seven years in South Wales, before transfer to Bristol in 1956 and finally to Old Oak Common, two weeks before this view. Withdrawal came on 28 September 1963. The station master's house can just be seen among the trees on the extreme left.

Forty years after closure, on 4 September 2006, all evidence of the station has vanished, although the station master's house still stands, out of sight to the left, now in private hands. To the right, the previous goods yard is now a vehicle dump and some of the items present can be seen approximately where the goods shed stood. Note the evidence of the re-railing with metal sleepers continuing on this side of the road bridge. *John Spencer Gilks/MJS*

MORETON-IN-MARSH was smaller than Stow, its southern neighbour on the A429 Roman Road, but was given a far greater presence by the OW&WR when the station opened on 4 June 1853, and its status was further enhanced by becoming a junction station on 1 July 1889, when a branch to Shipston-on-Stour opened on the route of the 1826 horse tramway known as the Stratford & Moreton Railway. Branch trains ran from a platform face on the outside of the up platform and the line for this can be seen curving away to the right in the distance of this shot from 7 July 1978. A mixture of two-thirds of a Class 119 three-car set and a Class 121 single unit leaves the station and heads south forming the 17.41 Worcester Foregate Street-Oxford service. In the down platform a Class 117 DMU has arrived as the 4.49pm service from Reading. The goods yard, on the extreme left, officially lost its services in the 1960s, but remained active for ad hoc freight duties, as seen here.

Much has changed over the past three decades, but much has remained the same. On 4 September 2006 the semaphores still stand as before, as does the controlling signal box. The former Shipston line still runs alongside the outer edge of the up platform, here occupied by a tamping machine, but now goes no further than the buffer stop immediately beyond. The main station building on the down platform survives, complete with canopy; and the goods shed is still in situ but not now rail-served. The extreme left-hand and right-hand sidings are the main casualties. Note the recent growth of new housing, upper right. *Michael Mensing/MJS*

MORETON-IN-MARSH: As if to prove that we authors do not only choose to include pretty pictures in glorious sunshine, here is a distinctly murky picture, but it has importance. Those of us of a certain age can remember the horrendous winter of 1947, but that of 1962/3 was a close second! With much of the country brought to a near

standstill with the frequent snow showers and freezing temperatures, it was left to the railways to continue when roads were so often virtually impassable. On Saturday 16 February 1963 an unidentified 'Grange' 4-6-0 is about to pass the station signal box as it makes a spirited restart from Moreton with the 10.20am Worcester-Oxford stopper. Your author remembers the date well, as he led a party of trainspotters around the sheds of the North East on this weekend, trying to avoid the 8-foot snowdrifts around some roads, travelling from shed to shed in a minibus!

Two decades later there is no snow but the weather is still unkind to the photographer! A lady shelters beneath her umbrella as she crosses the footbridge, which was by now open, unlike the covered one in the previous picture. The station buildings are unchanged apart from the loss of the chimney on the down (left) side, and the siding, barrow crossing, semaphore, signal box and station lighting are still the same, but the motive power is now completely steam-less! On 6 April 1982 DMU set L411, with Pressed Steel Class 117 DMS W51388 leading, makes a less obvious effort as it leaves forming the 1330 Hereford-Reading service.

After another two decades, on 4 September 2006 there are relatively minor changes. The view to the left is now restricted – the weedkilling train has obviously not been recently! – but incredibly, in these overly safety-conscious days, the barrow crossing remains in place. The signal box nameplate has reverted to white on black (see the centre picture) and the box itself has had its windows replaced and the wooden superstructure painted grey. Tree growth that seemed to have disappeared in the centre view has made a comeback; and there is yet another new footbridge, this time with a ramp for the disabled. The tamper glimpsed on the previous page is now seen more clearly. *Alan Donaldson/Tom Heavyside/MJS*

124

MORETON-IN-MARSH: Our last look at Moreton takes us on to the up platform on 24 April 1955, to witness No 5971 *Merevale Hall* entering the station with the 11.17am train for Oxford. The delights of the station at this period are plain to see and would have provided a fitting welcome to visiting tourists arriving by train. The attractive brick building on the down platform, complete with its large protective canopy, replaced the original wooden facility at the end of the 19th century. At the date of this shot, the wooden waiting shelter on the up platform remains, but this too was replaced later, this time with a stone structure. Note the grounded coach on the down platform, providing freight facilities, and the impressive covered footbridge between the platforms. The Shipston branch platform is to the right.

Though still very active as a station on what is now called 'The Cotswold Line', developments and 'improvements' have changed the whole ambience of the site, and not for the better! On 4 September 2006 'Adelante' DMU No 180109 replicates the above arrival but in no way has the same appeal. However, the eager travellers will not worry unduly as they travel in comfort on their London-bound train. The basic station layout remains, together with the A429 road bridge in the distance, but together with the disappearance of the main station building's chimneys, virtually everything else has changed, including the up waiting shelter, footbridge (in response to disability legislation), lighting, seating, station garden and the ubiquitous car park on the left. *MJS collection/MJS*

BLOCKLEY: Another example of an attractive GWR wayside station, Blockley is here seen to advantage on a sunny 14 September 1963, with colourful platform gardens and brown and cream running in sign in addition to the signal box and goods shed. Adding to the overall canvas, the smart green-liveried D7035 is about to pass through non-stop with a Worcester-Paddington express. Note the tall signal between the two lines, giving clear sighting for approaching trains. Opened on 4 June 1853, the station was again in a rural 'no-man's land', actually a mile closer to Paxford to the north-east than Blockley to the south-west! Originally of wood, the replacement station buildings in the 1920s were of the same material, so by the time of closure on 3 January 1966 they were suffering from the elements.

It is hardly believable that this is the same vantage point, but the sign confirms it! Such has been the change here, not least with now just single track, that on 4 September 2006 it seems inconceivable that there was ever enough room for the double track and two platforms. The level crossing is now protected by automatic barriers and CCTV, and the only sign of life is a Kotmatsu PW170es 'road/railer'. The one saving grace, however, was a bumper crop of delicious blackberries! *John Spencer Gilks/MJS*

CHIPPING CAMPDEN: Our final view is of progressive and dramatic change once more. Two miles north of Blockley, Chipping Campden opened on 4 June 1853 as 'Mickleton', after a village some 2½ miles to the north! A sensible realisation that Chipping Campden was both closer (only a mile away to the west) and larger came soon after, when the name was changed to 'Campden'. This prevailed until February 1952, when 'Chipping' was added, almost too late to be of any practical use! The station site is just visible through the arch of the large wooden goods shed as D7040 hauls another Worcester-Paddington express, this time on 12 October 1963. The goods shed and yard had closed three months earlier and already the grass is overtaking the siding.

Just six months later reclamation and demolition are the order of the day in the goods yard. Track has been lifted, with sleepers piled on the goods platform, and the shed is being systematically taken down. In something of a reversal of what might be expected, we see steam at this later date! On a decidedly dull 11 April 1964, No 7201, built to haul heavy freights, has something of a lighter load than its capabilities as it pulls away from the station site with a rake of unfitted wagons. Note the tall trees and tall building common to both views.

Thirty-two years later the transformation is complete. The station has completely disappeared, the old goods yard is now completely fenced off from a scrapyard, the track has been singled and the previous backdrop of trees and buildings has changed. The trees were removed, but new ones appear to be taking their place, while the industrial buildings have seen change. Only the middle one in the previous picture is as before, with the curved one without its roof and the taller one much reduced in height. The Campden & Chorleywood Food Research Association occupies the site on 4 September 2006. *Millbrook House collection/ Bryan Hicks/MJS*

INDEX OF LOCATIONS